# Learning Node.js for .NET Developers

Solve practical real-world problems using JavaScript and Node.js

**Harry Cummings**

PUBLISHING

BIRMINGHAM - MUMBAI

# Learning Node.js for .NET Developers

First published: June 2016

Production reference: 1170616

Published by Packt Publishing Ltd.
Livery Place
35 Livery Street
Birmingham B3 2PB, UK.

ISBN 978-1-78528-009-2

www.packtpub.com

# Credits

**Author**
Harry Cummings

**Reviewer**
David Simons

**Commissioning Editor**
Kunal Parikh

**Acquisition Editor**
Rahul Nair

**Content Development Editor**
Trusha Shriyan

**Technical Editor**
Jayesh Sonawane

**Copy Editor**
Safis Editing

**Project Coordinator**
Kinjal Bari

**Proofreader**
Safis Editing

**Indexer**
Mariammal Chettiyar

**Graphics**
Disha Haria

**Production Coordinator**
Nilesh Mohite

**Cover Work**
Nilesh Mohite

# About the Author

**Harry Cummings** has been working in software development for 8 years, and for the past few years, he has performed the role of technical lead across a variety of projects for varied clients. He has, in the past, also worked as a developer, project manager, and consultant. This gives him an excellent all-round view of the role of a technical lead and its relationship with other roles as well as insight into every stage of project delivery, from initial analysis to long-term maintenance.

Harry has extensive experience in C#/.NET, Java and Scala, and JavaScript/ Node.js. He continues to work directly with these technologies on a regular basis in the teams that he leads. His broader interests and expertise lie in sharing and nurturing software development best practices through training and mentoring. He has appeared at conferences such as NDC London and SDD Conf, speaking about diverse topics, ranging from introductory Node.js through to automated test strategies and long-term project maintainability.

# About the Reviewer

**David Simons** is a London-based software consultant. He is familiar with a wide range of tools, having helped clients such as the BBC and News International deliver web solutions in a range of languages, including .NET, Java, and full-stack JavaScript. He shares his insights around these and his background in statistics research at a range of conferences, including NDC and JSConf.

As of 2016, he works with London-based consultancy GraphAware to advocate and consult on the use of graph databases in modern applications.

# www.PacktPub.com

## eBooks, discount offers, and more

Did you know that Packt offers eBook versions of every book published, with PDF and ePub files available? You can upgrade to the eBook version at `www.PacktPub.com` and as a print book customer, you are entitled to a discount on the eBook copy. Get in touch with us at `customercare@packtpub.com` for more details.

At `www.PacktPub.com`, you can also read a collection of free technical articles, sign up for a range of free newsletters and receive exclusive discounts and offers on Packt books and eBooks.

`https://www2.packtpub.com/books/subscription/packtlib`

Do you need instant solutions to your IT questions? PacktLib is Packt's online digital book library. Here, you can search, access, and read Packt's entire library of books.

## Why subscribe?

- Fully searchable across every book published by Packt
- Copy and paste, print, and bookmark content
- On demand and accessible via a web browser

# Table of Contents

# Preface

The purpose of this book is to help .NET or Java developers make the leap to Node.js. You may have some web development experience, and perhaps you've written some browser-based JavaScript in the past. It might not be obvious why anyone would want to take JavaScript out of the browser and use it for server-side development. However, this is exactly what Node.js does. What's more, Node.js has been around for long enough now to have matured as a platform, and has sustained its impressive growth in popularity well beyond any period that could be attributed to initial hype over a new technology.

The first objective of this book then is to explain why Node.js is a compelling technology that's worth learning more about. The first few chapters introduce Node.js with this in mind, quickly get you up and running with Node.js, and provide an important (re) introduction to the JavaScript language to set you on the right track.

The main part of this book will then take you through a worked example of building up a Node.js web-application step by step. In the process, we'll illustrate all the important tools and techniques required for real-world development projects in Node.js. The aim is to make the most of your existing development expertise to allow you to quickly reach the same level of best practices and professionalism with Node.js.

The final chapters of the book show how to use Node.js for other purposes outside of web applications and how to continue learning Node.js and exploring the ecosystem around it. We'll also see how you can use Node.js alongside .NET and benefit from applying your programming skills across both technologies.

# What this book covers

*Chapter 1, Why Node.js?*, introduces Node.js as a programming platform. It covers the execution model of Node.js, particularly how it differs from .NET and Java, and the use cases in which these differences become strengths. This chapter also discusses the suitability of JavaScript as a development language.

*Chapter 2, Getting Started with Node.js*, dives straight into creating a Node.js application. In this chapter, you will install Node.js, choose a code editor, and set up a minimal web application project. You'll also learn some important command-line tools for working with Node.js.

*Chapter 3, A JavaScript Primer*, introduces the most important things to know when programming in JavaScript. It describes the JavaScript type system and its particular flavor of functional object-oriented programming, including prototype-based inheritance. This chapter also covers a few key gotchas and JavaScript language quirks.

*Chapter 4, Introducing Node.js Modules*, explains how to structure JavaScript applications using modules. It introduces the Node.js module system and shows you how to use this to organise your application's code.

*Chapter 5, Creating Dynamic Websites*, expands on the examples from the previous chapter to build a functioning web application. You'll add a JSON API and dynamic views to your application and communicate between the client and server using Ajax.

*Chapter 6, Testing Node.js Applications*, shows you how to write automated tests in JavaScript and Node.js. It introduces a number of tools and libraries for writing and running tests in JavaScript, and guides you through writing a variety of unit tests and integration tests for your application.

*Chapter 7, Setting up an Automated Build*, covers build automation and continuous integration in Node.js. You'll set up a CI server and task runner for your application, adding automated tasks to run tests, execute static analysis, and assess code coverage.

*Chapter 8, Mastering Asynchronicity*, introduces different patterns for asynchronous programming in JavaScript. You'll apply these to your own application and make the most of JavaScript language features and libraries for simplifying asynchronous code.

*Chapter 9, Persisting Data*, explains persistent data stores that can be used with Node.js. It introduces MongoDB and Redis, explaining their different data models and their use cases. You'll integrate both of these data stores with your Node.js application.

*Chapter 10, Creating Real-time Web Apps*, shows how to implement real-time two-way communication between the client and the server. You'll use the Socket.IO library to add real-time functionality into your application. You'll also see how to write tests for this functionality and how to write scalable real-time applications using Redis as a backend.

*Chapter 11, Deploying Node.js Applications*, demonstrates how to get a Node.js application onto the Web. You'll deploy your application to a free cloud-hosting provider. You'll see how to configure data stores and how to use remote server logs for debugging.

*Chapter 12, Authentication in Node.js*, covers authentication for Node.js web applications. You'll implement authentication using third-party providers, integrate this with your application, and show different content to logged-in and logged-out users.

*Chapter 13, Creating JavaScript Packages*, explains how to create standalone JavaScript packages for use by others. You'll see how to write universal JavaScript libraries that can run on both the client and the server, and how to write a standalone command-line application using Node.js.

*Chapter 14, Node.js and Beyond*, puts the content of this book in a wider context. It explains how Node.js and JavaScript are continuing to evolve, so you can be prepared for and take advantage of upcoming changes. It covers some alternative programming languages for Node.js and the Web, and how these relate to JavaScript. It discusses how some of the principles from Node.js can be applied to .NET programming, and illustrates how these are particularly visible in .NET Core (the new version of .NET). It also shows how you can use Node.js together with .NET to gain the best of both worlds.

# What you need for this book

All of the tools and services used in this book are available for free online. Most of the worked examples require an active web connection at some point. To get started, you need nothing more than a console, a web browser, and permission to install new software on your machine. To support developers coming from a .NET background, some of the console listings or example steps in this book use Windows conventions (for example, backslashes in paths). None of the examples depend on Windows specifically though. You can work through this book on Windows, Mac OSX, or Linux.

# Who this book is for

This book is for .NET or Java developers who are interested in learning Node.js. No prior experience with Node.js is expected. You might have written some client-side JavaScript before, but this is not required. The main worked example in this book is a Node.js web application. Web development experience in .NET or Java will be helpful, but it's not necessary to have experience with any particular application library or framework.

# Conventions

In this book, you will find a number of text styles that distinguish between different kinds of information. Here are some examples of these styles and an explanation of their meaning.

Code words in text, database table names, folder names, filenames, file extensions, pathnames, dummy URLs, user input, and Twitter handles are shown as follows: "ES2015 introduces the `let` keyword for declaring variables."

A block of code is set as follows:

```
<!DOCTYPE html>
<html>
  <head>
    <title>{{ title }}</title>
    <link rel='stylesheet' href='/stylesheets/style.css' />
  </head>
  <body>
    <h1>{{ title }}</h1>
    <p>Welcome to {{ title }}</p>
  </body>
</html>
```

When we wish to draw your attention to a particular part of a code block, the relevant lines or items are set in bold:

```
/* GET home page. */
router.get('/', function(req, res, next) {
  res.render('index', { title: 'Express', name: 'World' });
});
```

Any command-line input or output is written as follows:

```
> npm install -g nodemon
```

**New terms** and **important words** are shown in bold. Words that you see on the screen, for example, in menus or dialog boxes, appear in the text like this: "Clicking the **Next** button moves you to the next screen."

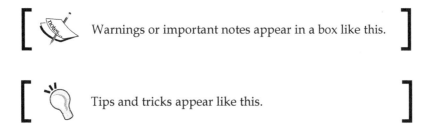

Warnings or important notes appear in a box like this.

Tips and tricks appear like this.

# Reader feedback

Feedback from our readers is always welcome. Let us know what you think about this book—what you liked or disliked. Reader feedback is important for us as it helps us develop titles that you will really get the most out of.

To send us general feedback, simply e-mail feedback@packtpub.com, and mention the book's title in the subject of your message.

If there is a topic that you have expertise in and you are interested in either writing or contributing to a book, see our author guide at www.packtpub.com/authors.

# Customer support

Now that you are the proud owner of a Packt book, we have a number of things to help you to get the most from your purchase.

# Downloading the example code

You can download the example code files for this book from https://github.com/NodeJsForDevelopers and also from your account at http://www.packtpub.com. If you purchased this book elsewhere, you can visit http://www.packtpub.com/support and register to have the files e-mailed directly to you.

You can download the code files by following these steps:

1. Log in or register to our website using your e-mail address and password.
2. Hover the mouse pointer on the **SUPPORT** tab at the top.
3. Click on **Code Downloads & Errata**.
4. Enter the name of the book in the **Search** box.
5. Select the book for which you're looking to download the code files.
6. Choose from the drop-down menu where you purchased this book from.
7. Click on **Code Download**.

You can also download the code files by clicking on the **Code Files** button on the book's webpage at the Packt Publishing website. This page can be accessed by entering the book's name in the **Search** box. Please note that you need to be logged in to your Packt account.

Once the file is downloaded, please make sure that you unzip or extract the folder using the latest version of:

- WinRAR / 7-Zip for Windows
- Zipeg / iZip / UnRarX for Mac
- 7-Zip / PeaZip for Linux

# Downloading the color images of this book

We also provide you with a PDF file that has color images of the screenshots/ diagrams used in this book. The color images will help you better understand the changes in the output. You can download this file from `http://www.packtpub.com/sites/default/files/downloads/LearningNodejsForNETDevelopers_ColorImages.pdf`.

# Errata

Although we have taken every care to ensure the accuracy of our content, mistakes do happen. If you find a mistake in one of our books—maybe a mistake in the text or the code—we would be grateful if you could report this to us. By doing so, you can save other readers from frustration and help us improve subsequent versions of this book. If you find any errata, please report them by visiting http://www.packtpub.com/submit-errata, selecting your book, clicking on the **Errata Submission Form** link, and entering the details of your errata. Once your errata are verified, your submission will be accepted and the errata will be uploaded to our website or added to any list of existing errata under the Errata section of that title.

To view the previously submitted errata, go to https://www.packtpub.com/books/content/support and enter the name of the book in the search field. The required information will appear under the **Errata** section.

# Piracy

Piracy of copyrighted material on the Internet is an ongoing problem across all media. At Packt, we take the protection of our copyright and licenses very seriously. If you come across any illegal copies of our works in any form on the Internet, please provide us with the location address or website name immediately so that we can pursue a remedy.

Please contact us at copyright@packtpub.com with a link to the suspected pirated material.

We appreciate your help in protecting our authors and our ability to bring you valuable content.

# Questions

If you have a problem with any aspect of this book, you can contact us at questions@packtpub.com, and we will do our best to address the problem.

# 1
# Why Node.js?

Node.js is still relatively new compared to platforms such as .NET and Java, but has become very popular in a short time, and has even started influencing these platforms. This is thanks to its distinctive programming model, extensive ecosystem, and powerful tooling.

These factors make Node.js a compelling alternative to other platforms. They can also make it intimidating. Its distinctive programming model may seem quite alien compared to other platforms. The sheer range of available libraries and tools can be bewildering.

This book will guide you through Node.js so you can start using it in your applications. It will help you to understand Node.js, navigate its ecosystem, and leverage your existing development skills in this new environment.

In this chapter, we will cover the following topics:

- Introducing the Node.js platform
- Seeing how its execution model works
- Exploring the Node.js ecosystem
- Looking at JavaScript as a language choice
- Considering the range of use cases for Node.js

## What is Node.js?

Node.js consists of a JavaScript engine together with low-level APIs for core server-side functionality. The execution engine is the same V8 engine developed for the Chrome web browser. Node.js takes this engine and embeds it in a standalone application that can run JavaScript outside the browser.

In Node.js, the standard APIs found in browsers to support client-side web development, such as the **Document Object Model (DOM)** and `XMLHttpRequest`, are not present. Instead, there are APIs to support general-purpose application development. These core APIs cover low-level functionality such as the following:

- Networking and security
- Accessing the file system
- Defining and requiring modules
- Raising and consuming events
- Handling binary data streams
- Compression
- UTF-8 support
- Retrieving basic information about the OS
- Managing child processes

Some of these APIs may already be familiar from developing client-side JavaScript. For example, the Timers API exposes the familiar `setTimeout` and `setInterval` functions.

Node.js also provides several tools to help with the development process. These include console logging, debugging, a **Read-Eval-Print Loop (REPL)** (or interactive console), and basic assertions for testing.

# Understanding the Node.js execution model

The execution model of Node.js follows that of JavaScript in the browser. It is quite different from that of most general-purpose programming platforms.

Stated formally, Node.js has a single-threaded, non-blocking, event-driven execution model. We will define each of these terms in this section.

# Non-blocking

Put simply, Node.js recognizes that many programmes spend most of their time waiting for other things to happen, for example, slow I/O operations such as disk access and network requests.

Node.js addresses this by making these operations non-blocking. This means that program execution can continue while they happen. For example, the filesystem API's stat function for retrieving statistics about a file may be called as follows:

```
fs.stat('/hello/world', function (error, stats) {
  console.log('File last updated at: ' + stats.mtime);
});
```

Two arguments are passed to the fs.stat function: the name of the file that we are interested in, and a **callback function**. The fs.stat call returns immediately, returning control of execution to the current thread but not returning a value. If there are further commands following the fs.stat call, these will then be executed. Otherwise, the thread is released to perform other work. The callback function is invoked (that is 'called back') only after the runtime has finished communicating with the filesystem. The result of the filesystem operation is passed into the callback function.

This non-blocking approach is also called **asynchronous** programming. Other platforms support this (for example, C#'s async/await keywords and .NET's Task Parallel Library). However, it is baked in to Node.js in a way that makes it simple and natural to use. Asynchronous API methods are all called in the same way as fs.stat. They all take a callback function that gets passed error and result arguments.

# Event-driven

The event-driven nature of Node.js describes how operations are scheduled. In typical procedural environments, a program has an entry point that executes a set of commands until completion, or enters a loop and performs some processing on each iteration.

Node.js has a built-in **event loop**, which isn't exposed to the developer. It is the job of the event loop to decide which piece of code to execute next. Typically, this will be a callback function that is ready to run in response to some other event. For example, a filesystem operation may have completed, a timeout may have expired, or a new network request may have arrived.

This built-in event loop simplifies asynchronous programming by providing a consistent approach and avoiding the need for applications to manage their own scheduling.

# Single-threaded

The single-threaded nature of Node.js simply means that there is only one thread of execution in each process. Also, each piece of code is guaranteed to run to completion without being interrupted by other operations. This greatly simplifies development and makes programs easier to reason about. It removes the possibility for a range of concurrency issues. For example, it is not necessary to synchronize/lock access to shared in-process state as it is in Java or .NET. A process can't deadlock itself or create race conditions within its own code. Single-threaded programming is only feasible if the thread never gets blocked waiting for long-running work to complete. Thus, this simplified programming model is made possible by the non-blocking nature of Node.js.

# Introducing the Node.js ecosystem

The built-in Node.js APIs provide a low-level core for creating applications. Applications typically only use a small number of these APIs directly. They often use third-party library modules that provide higher-level abstractions for application development.

Node.js has its own package manager, **npm**. This is similar to .NET's NuGet or the package management aspects of Java's Maven. Applications specify their dependencies in a simple JSON file.

The **npm registry** provides a central repository for packages. This registry has grown rapidly and is already much larger (in terms of number of available packages) than the corresponding repositories for other platforms (see http://www.modulecounts.com/). There are hundreds of thousands of packages available, providing a vast array of functionality.

The **npm command line tool** can be used to download packages and install new ones. Library dependencies are installed locally to each application. Some packages provide command-line tools, which may be installed globally rather than under a specific project.

Many frameworks available on npm are split into a small extensible core and a number of composable modules. This approach makes it easy to understand the libraries on which your application depends, avoiding the need to reason about complex heavyweight frameworks.

The consistency of calling non-blocking (asynchronous) API methods in Node.js carries through to its third-party libraries. This consistency makes it easy to build applications that are asynchronous throughout.

# Why JavaScript?

JavaScript is a language that can seem unintuitive compared to other popular **object-oriented (OO)** languages. It also has a number of quirks and flaws that have drawn criticism (and occasional ridicule). It might then seem a surprising choice of language for a new programming platform. This section discusses the factors that make JavaScript a more appealing choice.

## A clear canvas

The size and complexity of JavaScript is part of its appeal. The core language itself, which doesn't include APIs such as the DOM, is small and simple. This makes it easy for Node.js to establish its own styles and conventions.

The new APIs provided by Node.js and the consistent approach to asynchronous programming wouldn't be possible in a more complex language with a larger pre-existing standard class library.

## Functional nature

JavaScript was first built as a programming language for client-side functionality in the browser. This might not make it an obvious choice for general-purpose programming.

In fact, these two use cases do have something important in common. User interface code is naturally event-driven (for example, binding event handlers to button clicks). Node.js makes this a virtue by applying an event-driven approach to general-purpose programming.

JavaScript supports functions as first-class objects. This means it's easy to create functions dynamically and pass around references to them. This fits in well with the asynchronous, non-blocking approach of Node.js. In particular, it's easy to expose and use APIs based around callback functions.

## A bright future

JavaScript has received a lot of attention in the last several years as it has become more widely used for providing rich functionality on the Web. Browser vendors have put a huge amount of engineering effort into improving the performance of JavaScript. Node.js benefits from this directly via its use of Chrome's V8 engine.

The JavaScript language itself is undergoing some major changes for the better. The ECMAScript 2015 standard (previously known as ES6) represents the most significant revision of the language in its history. It introduces features that make the language more intuitive and less verbose. It also addresses flaws that JavaScript has been criticized for in the past, removing gotchas and making programs easier to reason about.

# When to use Node.js

As discussed earlier in this chapter, Node.js recognizes that I/O is a bottleneck for many applications. On most programming platforms, threads will waste time blocking on I/O operations. There are approaches developers can take to avoid this, but these all involve adding some complexity to their code. In Node.js, the platform itself provides a completely natural approach.

# Writing web applications

The flagship use case for Node.js is building web applications. These are inherently event-driven as most or all processing takes place in response to HTTP requests. Also, many websites do little computational heavy-lifting of their own. They tend to perform a lot of I/O operations:

- Streaming requests from the client
- Talking to a database, locally or over the network
- Pulling in data from remote APIs over the network
- Reading files from disk to send back to the client

These factors make I/O operations a likely bottleneck for web applications. The non-blocking programming model of Node.js allows web applications to make the most of a single thread. As soon as any of these I/O operations starts, the thread is immediately free to pick up and start processing another request. Processing of each request continues via asynchronous callbacks when I/O operations complete. The processing thread is only kicking off and linking together these operations, never waiting for them to complete. This allows Node.js to handle a much higher rate of requests per thread than other platforms. You can also still make use of multiple threads (for example, on multi-core CPUs) by simply running multiple instances of the Node.js process.

# Identifying other use cases

There are of course some applications that don't perform much I/O and are more likely to be CPU bound. Node.js would be less suitable for computationally-intensive applications. Programs that do a lot of processing of in-memory data are less concerned about I/O.

Web applications are not the only I/O-heavy applications though. Other classes of program that could be a good candidate for Node.js include the following:

- Tools that manipulate large amounts of data on disk
- Supervisor programs coordinating other software or hardware
- Non-browser GUI applications that need to respond to user input

Node.js is especially suitable for *glue* applications that pull together functionality from other remote services. The increasing popularity of microservices as an architectural pattern makes this kind of application more common.

# Why now?

Node.js has been around for several years, but now is the perfect time to start using it if you haven't already.

The release of Node.js v4 towards the end of 2015 consolidated the project's governance model and heralds Node.js coming to maturity. It also allows the project to keep more up to date with the V8 engine. This means that Node.js can benefit more directly from ongoing development on V8. For example, security and performance improvements to V8 will now make their way into Node.js much sooner.

As discussed earlier in this chapter, the release of the ECMAScript 2015 standard makes JavaScript a much more appealing language. It pulls in useful features from other popular OO languages and resolves a number of long-standing flaws in JavaScript.

Meanwhile, the ecosystem of third party libraries and tools around Node.js and JavaScript continues to grow. Node.js is treated as a first-class citizen by major hosting platforms. Companies such as Google and Microsoft are also throwing their weight behind JavaScript and related technologies.

# Summary

In this chapter, we have understood Node.js and its distinctive execution model, explored the growing ecosystem around Node.js and JavaScript, seen the reasons for JavaScript as a language choice, and described the kinds of application that can benefit from Node.js.

Now that you know how Node.js works and when to use it, it's time to dive in and get our first Node.js application up and running.

# 2
# Getting Started with Node.js

This chapter will get you up and running with Node.js. You'll see how quick this can be and how easy it is to start writing web applications. You'll also choose a development environment for working with Node.js. In this chapter, we will cover the following topics:

- Installing Node.js
- Writing our first Node.js web application
- Setting up our development environment

## Installing and running Node.js

To install Node.js, visit `https://nodejs.org`, and download and run the installer package for the currently recommended version. The examples in this book are based on Node.js v6, released in April 2016 and supported through to April 2018.

After installation, open up a console window (run command prompt on Windows, or terminal on Mac) and type `node`.

This opens the Node.js REPL, which works like the JavaScript console in browsers. Try typing in a few commands and see the output:

```
> function square(x) { return x*x; }
undefined
> square(42)
1764
> new Date()
2016-05-02T16:08:41.915Z
> var foo = { bar: 'baz' }
undefined
```

```
> typeof foo
'object'
> foo.bar
'baz'
```

Now let's make use of one of the Node.js-specific APIs to create an HTTP server. Type the following commands into the REPL (the output of each command is omitted from the listing below for brevity):

```
> var listener = function(request, response) { response.end('Hello World!') }
> require('http').createServer(listener).listen(3000)
```

Now try visiting `http://localhost:3000` in your browser. Congratulations! You have written your first web server, in just two lines of code. The first line defines a callback function for handling HTTP requests and returning a response. The second line sets up a new server that accepts HTTP requests on port 3000 and invokes our callback function for each request.

You can exit the Node.js REPL by typing `process.exit()`.

# Choosing an editor

Of course, we're not going to write all of our code inside the REPL. You can use any text editor or IDE you like for writing JavaScript for Node.js. If you're not sure what to use, try one of the following:

- Atom (`https://atom.io/`)
- Visual Studio Code (`https://code.visualstudio.com/`)

These are both free, lightweight IDEs that are actually implemented in Node.js. They are both available for Windows, Mac, and Linux.

The code listings in the rest of this book will be JavaScript source code files, not commands to be typed into the REPL.

# Using an application framework

The server we created in the REPL used the low-level HTTP module built into Node. js. This provides an API for creating a server that reads data from requests and writes to responses.

As with other programming platforms, there are frameworks available providing more useful high-level abstractions for writing web applications. These include things such as URL routing and templating engines. ASP.NET MVC, Ruby on Rails, and Spring MVC are all examples of such frameworks on different platforms.

**Example code**

If you get stuck at any point in this book, you can follow along with the code at `https://github.com/NodeJsForDevelopers` (there is a repository for each chapter and a commit for each heading that introduces any new code).

In this book, we'll be using a framework called Express to write a web application in Node.js. Express is the most popular web application framework for Node.js. It is well suited to small-scale applications such as the one we'll be building. It also provides a good introduction to important concepts. Most other popular Node.js web application frameworks are conceptually similar to Express, and several are actually built on top of it.

# Getting started with Express

To get our Express-based application started, we'll use npm to install the `express-generator` package, which will create a skeleton application based on Express. Run the following command in the console (that is, your regular terminal, not inside the Node.js REPL):

```
> npm install -g express-generator@~4.x
```

The `-g` option installs the Express generator globally, so you can run it from anywhere. The next command we run will create a new folder to contain our application code, so run this command wherever you want this folder to reside:

```
> express --hogan chapter02
```

**Templating engines**

Express offers a choice of templating engines. We'll be using Hogan, which is an implementation of the Mustache templating engine. You may already be familiar with Mustache from client-side libraries. Don't worry if not, though. It's very simple to pick up.

As you can see from the output, this sets up a minimal standard application structure for us. Now run the following command (as instructed by the generator output) to install the modules on which our application depends:

```
> cd chapter02
> npm install
```

The generator has created a skeleton Node.js web application for us. Let's try running this:

```
> npm start
```

Now visit `http://localhost:3000` again and you'll see the Express welcome page as shown here:

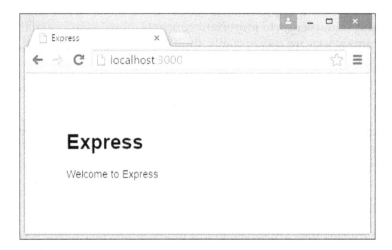

# Exploring our Express application

Let's look at the folders that the Express generator created for us:

- `node_modules`: This folder contains the third-party packages that our application depends on, which are installed when we run `npm install` (it is common to exclude this directory from source control)

- `public`: This folder contains the static assets of our application: images, client-side JavaScript, and CSS

- `routes`: This folder contains the logic of our application

- `views`: This folder contains the server-side templates for our application

There are also some files that aren't contained in any of the preceding folders:

- `package.json`: This file contains metadata about our application used by the `npm install` and `npm start` commands used earlier. We'll explore this file further in *Chapter 4, Introducing Node.js Modules*.

- `app.js`: This file is the main entry point for our application, which glues together all of the preceding components and initializes Express. We'll go through this file in more detail later on in this chapter.

- `bin/www`: This file is a Node.js script that launches our application. This is the script that gets executed when we run `npm start`.

It's not important to understand everything in the `bin/www` script at this point. However, note that it uses the same `http.createServer` call as in the REPL example before. This time, though, the listener argument is not a simple function but is our entire application (defined in `app.js`).

# Understanding Express routes and views

**Routes** in Express contain the logic for handling requests and rendering the appropriate response. They have similar responsibilities to controllers in MVC frameworks such as ASP.NET, Spring MVC, or Ruby on Rails.

The route that serves the page we just viewed in the browser can be found at `routes/index.js` and looks like this:

```
var express = require('express');
var router = express.Router();

/* GET home page. */
router.get('/', function(req, res, next) {
  res.render('index', { title: 'Express' });
});

module.exports = router;
```

The `require` call imports the Express module. We will discuss how this works in much more detail in *Chapter 4, Introducing Node.js Modules*. For now, think of it like a `using` or `import` statement in .NET or Java. The call to `express.Router()` creates a context under which we can define new routes. We will discuss this in more detail later on in this chapter (see *Creating modular applications with Express*). The `router.get()` call adds a new handler to this context for GET requests to the path `'/'`.

The `callback` function takes a request and response argument, similar to the listener in our "Hello World!" server at the beginning of this chapter. However, the request and response in this case are objects provided by Express, with additional functionality.

The `render` function allows us to respond with a template, which is rendered using the data we pass to it. This is typically the last thing you will do in a route's `callback` function. Here, we pass an object containing the title *Express* to the view template.

The view template can be found at `views/index.hjs` and looks like this:

```
<!DOCTYPE html>
<html>
  <head>
    <title>{{ title }}</title>
    <link rel='stylesheet' href='/stylesheets/style.css' />
  </head>
  <body>
    <h1>{{ title }}</h1>
    <p>Welcome to {{ title }}</p>
  </body>
</html>
```

This is a Hogan template. As mentioned previously, Hogan is an implementation of Mustache, a very lightweight templating language that limits the amount of logic in views. You can see the full syntax of Mustache at `https://mustache.github.io/mustache.5.html`.

Our template is a simple HTML page with some special template tags. The `{{ title }}` tags are replaced with the title field from the data passed in by the route.

Let's change the heading in the view to include a name as well as a title. It should look like this:

```
<h1>Hello, {{ name }}!</h1>
```

Try reloading the page again. You should see the following:

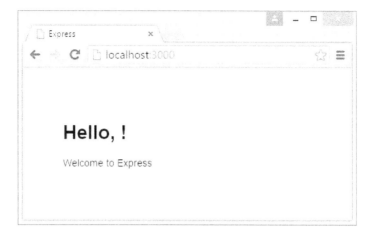

We don't have a name yet. That's because there is no **name** field in our view data. Let's fix that by editing our route:

```
var express = require('express');
var router = express.Router();

/* GET home page. */
router.get('/', function(req, res, next) {
  res.render('index', { title: 'Express', name: 'World' });
});

module.exports = router;
```

If we refresh our browser again at this point, we still won't see the name. That's because our application has already loaded our route, so won't pick up the change.

Go back to your terminal and kill the running application. Start it again (using npm start) and reload the page in the browser. You should now see the text **Hello, World!**.

# Using nodemon for automatic restarts

Restarting the application every time we make a change is a bit tedious. We can do better by running our application with **nodemon**, which will automatically restart the application whenever we make a change:

```
> npm install -g nodemon
> nodemon
```

Try updating the `routes/index.js` file again (for example, change the name string to your own name), then refresh the browser. This time, the change should appear without you needing to manually stop and restart the application. Note that the process is restarted by nodemon though, so if our application stored any internal state, this would be lost.

# Creating modular applications with Express

To find out how our route gets called when a request is made, we need to look at the `app.js` bootstrapping file. See the following two lines:

```
var routes = require('./routes/index');
...
app.use('/', routes);
```

This tells Express to use the routing context defined in `routes/index.js` for requests to the root path (`'/'`).

There is a similar call setting up a route under the `/users` path. Try visiting this path in your browser. The route that renders this response is defined in `/routes/users.js`.

Note that the route in `/routes/users.js` is *also* bound to `'/'`, the same as the route in `/routes/index.js`. The reason this works is that these paths are each relative to a separate Router instance, and the instance created in `/routes/users.js` is mounted under the `/users` path in `app.js`.

This mechanism makes it easy to build large applications composed from smaller modules. You can think of it as similar to the Areas functionality in ASP.NET MVC, or simply as an alternative structure to MVC controllers grouping together action methods.

# Bootstrapping an Express application

Let's take a look at the rest of the `app.js` file. Your file might not look identical to the listings below due to minor differences in our versions of Express, but it will contain broadly the same sections.

The various `require()` calls at the top of the file import the modules used by the application, including built-in Node.js modules (HTTP and Path), third-party libraries, and the application's own routes. The following lines initialize Express, telling it where to look for view templates and what rendering engine to use (in our case, Hogan):

```
var app = express();
// view engine setup
app.set('views', path.join(__dirname, 'views'));
app.set('view engine', '{views}');
```

The rest of the file consists of calls to `app.use()`. These register various different **middleware** for processing the request. The order in which they are registered forms a request processing pipeline. You might already be familiar with this pattern from servlet filters in Java, or the `IAppBuilder`/`IApplicationBuilder`/`IBuilder` interfaces in OWIN and ASP.NET. Don't worry if not though; we'll explore middleware thoroughly here.

# Understanding Express middleware

Middleware functions are the fundamental building blocks of an Express application. They are simply functions that take request and response arguments (just like our listener functions before) and a reference to the next middleware in the chain.

Each middleware function can manipulate the request and response objects before passing onto the next middleware in the chain. By chaining middleware together in this way, you can build complex functionality from simple modular components. It also allows clean separation between your application logic and cross-cutting concerns such as logging, authentication, or error handling.

Instead of passing control to the next middleware in the chain, a function can also end the processing of the request and return a response. Middleware can also be mounted to specific paths or router instances, for example, if we want enhanced logging on a particular part of our site.

In fact, Express routes are just another example of middleware: the routes that we have already looked at are ordinary middleware functions with the same three arguments noted above. They just happen to be mounted to a specific path and to return a response.

## Implementing error handling

Let's take a closer look at some of the middleware in `app.js`. First, look at the 404 error handler:

```
app.use(function(req, res, next) {
  var err = new Error('Not Found');
  err.status = 404;
  next(err);
});
```

This function always returns a response. So why do we not always get a 404 from our application? Remember that middleware is called in order, and the routes (which are registered before this function) return a response and don't call the next middleware. This means that the 404 function will only be called for requests that don't match any route, which is exactly what we want.

What about the other two error handlers in app.js? They return a 500 response with a custom error page. Why does our application not return a 500 response in all cases? How do these get executed if another middleware throws an error before calling `next()`?

Error-handling is a special case in Express. Error-handling middleware functions take four arguments instead of three, with the first parameter being an error. They should be registered last, after all other middlewares.

In the case of an error (either an error being thrown or a middleware function passing in an error argument when calling `next`), Express will skip any other non-error handling middleware and start executing the error handlers.

## Using Express middleware

Let's see some Express middleware in action by making use of cookie parsing middleware (which is already part of the skeleton application created by `express-generator`). We can do this by using a cookie to store how many times someone has visited the site. Update `routes/index.js` as follows:

```
router.get('/', function(req, res, next) {
  var visits = parseInt(req.cookies.visits) || 0;
  visits += 1;
  res.cookie('visits', visits);
  res.render('index',
      { title: 'Express', name: 'World', visits: visits }
  );
});
```

And add a new line to `views/index.hjs`:

```
<p>You have visited this site {{visits}} time(s).</p>
```

Now visit `http://localhost:3000/` again and refresh the page a few times. You should see the visit count increase based on the value stored in the cookie. To see what the cookie parsing middleware is doing for us, try deleting or commenting out the following line from `app.js` and reloading the page:

```
app.use(cookieParser());
```

As you can see from the error, the `cookies` property of the request is now undefined. The cookie parsing middleware looks at the cookie header of the request and turns it into a convenient JavaScript object for us. This is a common use case for middleware. The `bodyParser` middleware functions do a very similar job with the request body, turning raw text into a JavaScript object that is easier to use in our routes.

Note that the error response above also demonstrates our error handling middleware. Try commenting out the error handlers at the end of the `app.js` file and reloading the page again. We now get the default stack trace rather than the custom error response defined in our handler.

# Summary

In this chapter, we installed Node.js, saw how to interact with it from the command line, and started using it to write web applications. We learned about Express and how we can structure an application using routes and middleware.

Although we've seen some code in this chapter, we haven't really explored the JavaScript syntax in detail. Before adding more functionality to our application, we should make sure that we're up to speed with JavaScript. This is the subject of the next chapter.

# 3
# A JavaScript Primer

It's important to have a solid understanding of JavaScript to write Node.js applications. JavaScript is not a large or complex language, but it may seem unusual, and has a few quirks and gotchas to watch out for.

The recent release of ECMAScript 2015 (previously named ES6) introduces a number of new language features to make JavaScript programming easier and safer. Not all ES2015 features are available in all implementations yet. However, all the ES2015 features we'll mention in this chapter are available in Node.js and in most other JavaScript environments.

In this chapter, we'll familiarize ourselves with JavaScript so we can write Node.js applications with confidence. We will cover the following topics:

- The JavaScript type system
- JavaScript as a functional programming language
- Object-oriented programming in JavaScript
- JavaScript's prototype-based inheritance

## Introducing JavaScript types

JavaScript is a dynamically-typed language. These means that types are checked at runtime when you try to do something with a variable, rather than by a compiler. For example, the following is valid JavaScript code:

```
var myVariable = 0;
console.log(typeof myVariable); // Prints "number"
myVariable = "1";
console.log(typeof myVariable); // Prints "string"
```

Although variables do have a type, this may change throughout the lifetime of the variable.

JavaScript also tries to implicitly convert types where possible, for example, using the equality operator:

```
console.log(2 == "2"); // Prints "true"
```

Although this might make sense for frontend JavaScript (for example comparing against the value of a form input), in general, it is more likely to be a source of errors or confusion. For this reason, it is recommended to always use the strict equality and inequality operators:

```
console.log(2 === "2"); // Prints "false"
console.log(2 !== "2"); // Prints "true"
```

# JavaScript primitive types

JavaScript has a small number of primitive types, similar to C# and Java. These are string, number, and Boolean, as well as the special single-valued types, null and undefined. ES2015 also adds the symbol type, but we won't cover it here as its use cases are more advanced.

**Strings** are immutable, like in C# and Java. Concatenating strings creates a new string instance. String literals can be defined with double quotes (as in C# or Java) or single quotes. These can be used interchangeably (usually whatever is easier to avoid escaping).

ES2015 also introduces support for template strings, which are defined using backticks and can include interpolated expressions.

Here are several ways to define the same string:

```
var singleQuoted = '"Hey", I said, "I\'m a string"';
var doubleQuoted = "\"Hey\", I said, \"I'm a string\"";
console.log(doubleQuoted === singleQuoted); // Prints "true"

var expression = 'Hey';
var templated = `"${expression}", I said, "I'm a string"`;
console.log(templated === singleQuoted); // Prints "true"
```

**Number** is JavaScript's only built-in numeric type. It is a double-precision 64-bit floating-point number, like double in C# or Java. It has special values NaN (not a number) and Infinity for values that cannot be represented otherwise:

```
console.log(1 / 0); // Prints "Infinity"
console.log(Infinity + 1); // Prints "Infinity"
```

```
console.log((1 / 0) === (2 / 0)); // Prints "true"

var notANumber = parseInt("foo");
console.log(notANumber); // Prints "NaN"
console.log(notANumber === NaN); // Prints "false"
console.log(isNaN(notANumber)); // Prints "true"
```

 Note that although there is only a single NaN value, it is not treated as equal to itself. JavaScript provides the special isNaN function for testing whether a variable contains the NaN value.

The **null** type has a single instance, represented by the literal null, just as in C# or Java. JavaScript also has the **undefined** type. Variables or parameters that have never been assigned will have the value undefined:

```
var declared;
console.log(typeof declared); // Prints "undefined"
console.log(declared === undefined); // Prints "true"

console.log(typeof undeclared); // Prints "undefined"
console.log(undeclared === undefined); // throws ReferenceError
```

Note that our undeclared identifier cannot be accessed as a variable in normal code because it has not been declared. However, we can pass it to the typeof operator, which evaluates to the undefined type.

# Functional object-oriented programming

JavaScript is a functional object-oriented programming language. However, it is quite different to other object-oriented programming languages such as C# or Java. Despite having a similar syntax, there are some important differences.

## Functional programming in JavaScript

In JavaScript, functions are first-class objects. This means that functions can be treated like any other object: they can be created dynamically, assigned to variables, or passed into methods as arguments.

This makes it very easy to specify event callbacks, or to program in a more functional style using **higher-order functions**. Higher-order functions are functions that take other functions as arguments, and/or return another function. Here's a trivial example of filtering an array of numbers first in an imperative style and then in a functional style. Note that this example also shows JavaScript's **array literal notation** for creating arrays, using square brackets. It also demonstrates JavaScript's conditional construct and one of its loop constructs, which should be familiar from other languages:

```
var numbers = [1,2,3,4,5,6,7,8];

var filteredImperatively = [];
for (var i = 0; i < numbers.length; ++i) {
    var number = numbers[i];
    if (number % 2 === 0) {
        filteredImperatively.push(number);
    }
}
console.log(filteredImperatively); // Prints [2, 4, 6, 8]

var filteredFunctionally =
    numbers.filter(function(x) { return x % 2 === 0; });
console.log(filteredFunctionally); // Prints [2, 4, 6, 8]
```

The second approach in the example makes use of a function expression to define a new, anonymous function inline. In general, this is referred to as a lambda expression (after lambda calculus in mathematics). This function is passed-in to the built in `filter` expression available on JavaScript arrays.

In C#, assignment and passing of behavior was originally only possible using delegates. Since C# 3.0, support for lambda expressions makes it much easier to use functions in this way. This allows a more functional style of programming, for example, using C#'s **Language-Integrated Query** (**LINQ**) features.

In Java, for a long time there was no native way for a function to exist independently. You would have to define a method on a (possibly anonymous) class and pass this around, adding a lot of boilerplate. Java 8 introduces support for lambda expressions in a similar way to C#.

While C# and Java may have taken a while to catch up, you might be thinking that JavaScript is now falling behind. The syntax for defining a new function in JavaScript is quite clumsy compared to the lambda syntax in C# and Java.

This is especially unfortunate since JavaScript uses a C-like syntax for familiarity with other languages like Java! This is resolved in ES2015 with **arrow functions**, allowing us to rewrite the previous example as follows:

```
var numbers = [1,2,3,4,5,6,7,8];
var filteredFunctionally = numbers.filter(x => x % 2 === 0);
console.log(filteredFunctionally); // Prints [2, 4, 6, 8]
```

This is a simple arrow function with a single argument and a single expression. In this case, the expression is implicitly returned.

 It can be useful to read the => notation in arrow functions as *goes to*.

Arrow functions may have multiple (or zero) arguments, in which case they must be surrounded by parentheses. If the function body is enclosed in braces, it may contain multiple statements, in which case there is no implicit return. These are exactly the same syntax rules as for lambda expressions in C#.

Here is a more complex arrow function expression that returns the maximum of its two arguments:

```
var max = (a, b) => {
    if (a > b) {
        return a;
    } else {
        return b;
    }
};
```

# Understanding scopes in JavaScript

Traditionally, in JavaScript, there are only two possible variable scopes: global and functional. That is, an identifier (a variable name) is defined globally, or for an entire function. This can lead to some surprising behavior, for example:

```
function scopeDemo() {
    for (var i = 0; i < 10; ++i) {
        var j = i * 2;
    }
    console.log(i, j);
}
scopeDemo();
```

In most other languages, you would expect i to exist for the duration of the for loop, and j to exist for each loop iteration. You would therefore expect this function to log undefined undefined. In fact, it logs 10 18. This is because the variables are not scoped to the block of the for loop, but to the entire function. So the preceding code is equivalent to the following:

```
function scopeDemo() {
    var i, j;
    for (i = 0; i < 10; ++i) {
        j = i * 2;
    }
    console.log(i, j);
}
scopeDemo();
```

JavaScript treats all variable declarations as if they were made at the top of the function. This is known as **variable hoisting**. Although consistent, this can be confusing and lead to subtle bugs.

ES2015 introduces the let keyword for declaring variables. This works exactly the same as var except that variables are block-scoped. There is also the const keyword, which works the same as let except that it does not allow reassignment. It is recommended that you always use let rather than var, and use const wherever possible. Check the following code for example:

```
function scopeDemo() {
    "use strict";
    for (let i = 0; i < 10; ++i) {
        let j = i * 2;
    }
    console.log(i, j); // Throws ReferenceError: i is not defined
}
scopeDemo();
```

Note the "use strict" string in the preceding example. We'll discuss this in the next section.

## Strict mode

The "use strict" string is a hint to the JavaScript interpreter to enable **Strict Mode**. This makes the language safer by treating certain usages of the language as errors. For example, mistyping a variable name without strict mode will define a new variable at the global level, rather than causing an error.

Strict mode is also now used by some browsers to enable features in the newest version of JavaScript, such as the `let` and `const` keywords previously shown. If you are running these examples in a browser, you may find that the preceding listing doesn't work without strict mode.

In any case, you should always enable strict mode in all of your production code. The `"use strict"` string affects all code in the current scope (that is, JavaScript's traditional functional or global scope), so should usually be placed at the top of a function (or the top of a module's script file in Node.js).

# Object-oriented programming in JavaScript

Anything that is not one of JavaScript's built-in primitives (strings, number, null, and so on) is an **object**. This includes functions, as we've seen in the previous section. Functions are just a special type of object that can be invoked with arguments. Arrays are a special type of object with list-like behavior. All objects (including these two special types) can have properties, which are just names with a value. You can think of JavaScript objects as a dictionary with string keys and object values.

Objects can be created with properties using the object literal notation, as in the following example:

```
var myObject = {
    myProperty: "myValue",
    myMethod: function() {
        return `myProperty has value "${this.myProperty}"`;
    }
};
console.log(myObject.myMethod());
```

You might find this notation familiar even if you've never written any JavaScript, as it is the basis for JSON. Note that a method is just an object property that happens to have a function as its value. Also note that within methods, we can refer to the containing object using the `this` keyword.

Finally, note that we did not need to define a class for our object. JavaScript is unusual amongst object-oriented languages in that it doesn't really have classes.

## Programming without classes

In most object-oriented languages, we can declare methods in a class for use by all of its object instances. We can also share behavior between classes through inheritance.

Let's say we have a graph with a very large number of points. These may be represented by objects that are created dynamically and have some common behavior. We could implement points like this:

```
function createPoint(x, y) {
    return {
        x: x,
        y: y,
        isAboveDiagonal: function() {
            return this.y > this.x;
        }
    };
}

var myPoint = createPoint(1, 2);
console.log(myPoint.isAboveDiagonal()); // Prints "true"
```

One problem with this approach is that the isAboveDiagonal method is redefined for each point on our graph, thus taking up more space in memory.

We can address this using **prototypal inheritance**. Although JavaScript doesn't have classes, objects can inherit from other objects. Each object has a **prototype**. If we try to access a property on an object and that property doesn't exist, the interpreter will look for a property with the same name on the object's prototype instead. If it doesn't exist there, it will check the prototype's prototype, and so on. The prototype chain will end with the built-in Object.prototype.

We can implement this for our point objects as follows:

```
var pointPrototype = {
    isAboveDiagonal: function() {
        return this.y > this.x;
    }
};

function createPoint(x, y) {
    var newPoint = Object.create(pointPrototype);
    newPoint.x = x;
    newPoint.y = y;
    return newPoint;
}

var myPoint = createPoint(1, 2);
console.log(myPoint.isAboveDiagonal()); // Prints "true"
```

The `isAboveDiagonal` method now only exists once in memory, on the `pointPrototype` object.

When we try to call `isAboveDiagonal` on an individual point object, it is not present, but it is found on the prototype instead.

Note that this tells us something important about the `this` keyword. It actually refers to the object that the current function was called on, rather than the object it was defined on.

## Creating objects with the new keyword

We can rewrite the preceding code example in a slightly different form, as follows:

```
var pointPrototype = {
    isAboveDiagonal: function() {
        return this.y > this.x;
    }
}

function Point(x, y) {
    this.x = x;
    this.y = y;
}

function createPoint(x, y) {
    var newPoint = Object.create(pointPrototype);
    Point.apply(newPoint, arguments);
    return newPoint;
}

var myPoint = createPoint(1, 2);
```

This makes use of the special `arguments` object, which contains an array of the arguments to the current function. It also uses the `apply` method (which is available on all functions) to call the `Point` function on the `newPoint` object with the same arguments.

At the moment, our `pointPrototype` object isn't particularly closely associated with the `Point` function. Let's resolve this by using the `Point` function's `prototype` property instead. This is a built-in property available on all functions by default. It just contains an empty object to which we can add additional properties:

```
function Point(x, y) {
    this.x = x;
    this.y = y;
```

```
}

Point.prototype.isAboveDiagonal = function() {
    return this.y > this.x;
}

function createPoint(x, y) {
    var newPoint = Object.create(Point.prototype);
    Point.apply(newPoint, arguments);
    return newPoint;
}

var myPoint = createPoint(1, 2);
```

This might seem like a needlessly complicated way of doing things. However, JavaScript has a special operator that allows us to greatly simplify the previous code, as follows:

```
function Point(x, y) {
    this.x = x;
    this.y = y;
}

Point.prototype.isAboveDiagonal = function() {
    return this.y > this.x;
}

var myPoint = new Point(1, 2);
```

The behavior of the `new` operator is identical to our `createPoint` function in the previous example. There is one small exception: if the `Point` function actually returned a value, then this would be used instead of `newPoint`. It is conventional in JavaScript to start functions with a capital letter if they are intended to be used with the `new` operator.

## Programming with classes

Although JavaScript doesn't really have classes, ES2015 introduces a new `class` keyword. This makes it possible to implement shared behavior and inheritance in a way that may be more familiar compared to other object-oriented languages.

The equivalent of our preceding code would look like the following:

```
class Point {
    constructor(x, y) {
        this.x = x;
```

```
        this.y = y;
    }

    isAboveDiagonal() {
        return this.y > this.x;
    }
}

var myPoint = new Point(1, 2);
```

Note that this really is equivalent to our preceding code. The `class` keyword is just syntactic sugar for setting up the prototype-based inheritance already discussed.

## Class-based inheritance

As mentioned before, an object's prototype may in turn have another prototype, allowing a chain of inheritance. Setting up such a chain becomes quite complicated using the prototype-based approach from the previous section. It is much more intuitive using the class keyword, as in the following example (which might be used for plotting a graph with error bars):

```
class UncertainPoint extends Point {
    constructor(x, y, uncertainty) {
        super(x, y);
        this.uncertainty = uncertainty;
    }

    upperLimit() {
        return this.y + this.uncertainty;
    }

    lowerLimit() {
        return this.y - this.uncertainty;
    }
}

var myUncertainPoint = new Point(1, 2, 0.5);
```

# Summary

In this chapter, we have introduced JavaScript's type system, understood functions as first-class objects in JavaScript, seen how JavaScript differs from other object-oriented languages, implemented inheritance using prototypes and classes, and learned the new features of ECMAScript 2015 (ES6) that make the language safer and more intuitive to use.

Now that you have a firm grounding in JavaScript, you can start writing Node.js applications with confidence. In the next chapter, we will expand on our Express project and see how the module system in Node.js allows us to structure our codebase.

# Introducing Node.js Modules

Now that we're up to speed with the syntax of the JavaScript language, we can start building up our application. To do this, we need to know how to structure our application to allow it to grow in a maintainable way.

In this chapter, we will cover the following topics:

- Structuring JavaScript code with modules
- Declaring and using our own modules
- Organizing modules into files and directories
- Implementing an Express middleware module

## Organizing your codebase

Most programming platforms provide several mechanisms for structuring your code. Consider C#/.NET or Java: you can use classes, namespaces or packages, and compilation units (assemblies or JAR/WAR files). Notice the range from small-scale organizational units (classes) to large-scale ones (assemblies). This allows you to make a codebase more approachable by providing order at each level of detail.

Classic browser-based JavaScript development was quite unstructured. Functions were the only built-in language feature for organizing your code. You could split your code into separate script files, but these all share the same global context within a web page.

Over time, people have developed ways of organizing JavaScript code. The standard approach now is to use **modules**. There are a few different module systems available for JavaScript, but they all work in a similar way. Each module system includes the following aspects:

- A way of declaring a module with a name and its own scope
- A way of defining functionality provided by the module
- A way of importing a module into another script

In each system, when you import a module, you get a plain JavaScript object that you can assign to a variable. For most modules, this will be an object with several properties containing functions. But it could be any valid JavaScript object, for example, a single function.

Most module systems expect or at least encourage you to define each module in a separate file, just as you would with classes in other languages. It is also common for large modules to be composed of other, smaller, modules. These would be grouped together under the same directory. In this way, modules act more like namespaces or packages.

The flexibility of modules means that you can use them to structure your code at different scales. The lack of a built-in hierarchy of organizational units in JavaScript provides more flexibility. It also forces you to think more about how you structure your code.

# JavaScript module systems

ECMAScript 2015 introduces modules as a built-in feature of the language. They have been common practice for a while, though. For client-side programming, this practice has relied on using third-party libraries to provide a module system.

You may have seen RequireJS, which provides a way of using functions to define modules. RequireJS uses plain JavaScript and works in any environment. It is most useful in the browser, where additional modules may be loaded over the Internet. RequireJS addresses some of the pitfalls of loading additional scripts dynamically and asynchronously.

The Node.js environment has its own module system, which we will look at in the rest of this chapter. It makes use of the filesystem for organizing modules.

You might come across the terms **AMD** or **CommonJS**. These are standards for defining modules. RequireJS is an implementation of AMD, and Node.js modules follow the CommonJS standard. ECMAScript 2015 modules define a new standard with new `export` and `import` language keywords. The syntax is quite similar, though, to the Node.js module system we'll be using in this book, and it is easy to switch between the two.

# Creating modules in Node.js

We've actually already used several Node.js modules and created some of our own. Let's look again at our application from *Chapter 2, Getting Started with Node.js*.

The following code is from `routes/index.js` and `routes/users.js`:

```
module.exports = router;
```

The following is the code from `app.js`:

```
var express = require('express');
var path = require('path');
var favicon = require('serve-favicon');
var logger = require('morgan');
var cookieParser = require('cookie-parser');
var bodyParser = require('body-parser');

var routes = require('./routes/index');
var users = require('./routes/users');
```

Each of our routes (index and users) is a module. They expose their functionality using the built-in `module` object, which is defined by Node.js as a variable scoped to each module. In the preceding example, the object provided by each of our route modules is an Express router instance. The `app.js` script imports these modules using the built-in `require` function.

Observe that `app.js` also imports various npm packages using `require`. Note that it uses file paths to reference our own modules, whereas npm modules are referenced by name.

Let's look at how Node.js modules satisfy the three aspects of JavaScript module functionality.

# Declaring a module with a name and its own scope

In Node.js, each separate JavaScript file is automatically treated as a new module. Unlike scripts loaded into a web page, each file has its own scope. The name of the module is the name of the file.

# Defining functionality provided by the module

Node.js provides two built-in variables for exporting functionality from a module. These are `module.exports` and `exports`. `module.exports` is initialized to an empty object. `exports` is just a reference to `module.exports`. It is equivalent to the following appearing before your script:

```
var exports = module.exports = {};
```

Whatever is contained in the `module.exports` variable at the end of your script is the exported value of your module. This will be returned whenever your module is imported elsewhere. The following are all equivalent:

```
module.exports.foo = 1;
module.exports.bar = 2;

module.exports = { foo: 1, bar: 2 };

exports.foo = 1;
exports.bar = 2;
```

Note that the following is *not* the same as the previous examples. It just reassigns `exports`, but doesn't alter `module.exports` at all:

```
exports = { foo: 1, bar: 2 };
```

# Importing a module into another script

Node.js provides another built-in variable for importing modules. This is the `require` function we saw in `app.js` earlier in the chapter. This function is provided by Node.js and always available. It takes a single argument, which is the name or path of the module you want to import. The following excerpts from `app.js` demonstrate loading a third-party module by name and one of our own modules by a file path:

```
var express = require('express');
...
var routes = require('./routes/index');
```

Note that we don't need to specify the `.js` file extension for our own module. Node.js will automatically add this for us.

# Defining a directory-level module

As mentioned at the beginning of this chapter, modules can also act more like namespaces. We can treat a whole directory as a module, consisting of smaller modules in individual files. The simplest way to do this is to create an `index.js` file in the directory.

When calling `require('./directoryName')`, Node.js will attempt to load a file named `'./directoryName/index.js'` (relative to the current script). There is nothing special about `index.js` itself. This is just another script file that exposes an entry point to the module. If `directoryName` contains a `package.json` file, Node.js will load this file first and see if it specifies a `main` script, in which case Node.js will load this script instead of looking for `index.js`.

To import local modules, we use a file or directory path, that is, something starting with `'/'`, `'../'`, or `'./'` as in the preceding example. If we call `require` with a plain string, Node.js treats it as relative to the `node_modules` folder. The `npm` packages are just directory-level modules under this folder. We will look at defining our own `npm` packages in more detail in a later chapter.

# Implementing an Express middleware module

Let's return to the Node.js application we started in *Chapter 2*, *Getting Started with Node.js*. We're going to write an application where users can set puzzles for one another. First of all, we'll need a way of identifying the current user. We'll need to do this on most requests, making it a cross-cutting concern. This is a good use case for middleware.

For now, we will implement users in the simplest way possible, just storing an ID in a cookie. We will look into more robust identification in a later chapter. Note, however, that our use of middleware means it will be easy to alter our approach later on. This concern is encapsulated in our user middleware, so we only need to change it in one place.

First, we need a way of generating unique IDs. For this, we will use the UUID module from npm. We can add this to our project by running the following on the command line:

```
> npm install uuid --save
```

The --save flag stores the name of this module in our package.json file so that it will be installed automatically by npm install. This is useful for restoring our application from a clean checkout of the source code (recall that people commonly exclude the node_modules directory from source control, precisely because it can easily be restored in this way).

Now we are ready to create our middleware, which will place under middleware/users.js:

```
'use strict';

const uuid = require('uuid');

module.exports = function(req, res, next) {
    let userId = req.cookies.userId;
    if (!userId) {
        userId = uuid.v4();
        res.cookie('userId', userId);
    }
    req.user = {
        id: userId
    };
    next();
};
```

Notice that we use the ES2015 const keyword for the uuid module because this reference never changes. But we use the let keyword for the userId variable because this can be reassigned. Also notice that we call next() rather than returning a response, so the next middleware can continue processing the request.

Finally, we need to add this middleware to our application in app.js:

```
var users = require('./middleware/users');
var routes = require('./routes/index');
var app = express();

...

app.use(users);
```

```
app.use('/', routes);
```

```
. . .
```

Note that this replaces the import and usage of the `./routes/users` module that was generated for us. This route wasn't particularly useful, but we will add more routes soon.

We can check that our middleware works by altering our index route and view as follows:

```
routes/index.jsrouter.get('/', function(req, res, next) {
  res.render('index', { title: 'Welcome', userId: req.user.id });
});
```

The following is the code `views/index.hjs`:

```
<body>
  <h1>{{ title }}</h1>
  <p>Your user ID is {{ userId }}.</p>
</body>
```

Launch the application and visit `http://localhost:3000/`. You should see a randomly-generated user ID. Refresh the page and you should retain the same ID. Open the site in a different browser (or an incognito/private browsing window). This separate browser session should see a different ID.

# Summary

In this chapter, we have seen how to use Node.js modules to structure our codebase, and how to create an Express middleware module to implement cross-cutting concerns.

Now that we have a way of structuring our codebase and a means of identifying users, we can get on with implementing our application's functionality. In the next chapter, we'll start adding some interactivity to our application.

# 5
# Creating Dynamic Websites

Now that we have established a basic structure for our application, we can start to add more functionality and build a dynamic website that responds to user input.

In this chapter, we will cover the following topics:

- Adding a new module to our application for storing and deleting data
- Exposing a JSON API to handle user-submitted data
- Implementing communication between the client and server using Ajax
- Building up more complex HTML views using partial templates

## Handling user-submitted data

We're going to implement the classic guessing game of Hangman (see https://en.wikipedia.org/wiki/Hangman_(game)). Users will be able to post new words to guess, and to guess words posted by others. We'll look at creating new games first.

First, we'll add a new module for managing our games. For now, we'll just store our games in the memory. If we want to put games in some persistent storage in future, this is the module we will change. The interface (that is, the functions added to `module.exports`) can remain the same though.

We add the following code under `services/games.js`:

```
'use strict';

const games = [];
let nextId = 1;

class Game {
    constructor(id, setBy, word) {
```

```
            this.id = id;
            this.setBy = setBy;
            this.word = word.toUpperCase();
        }
    }

    module.exports.create = (userId, word) => {
        const newGame = new Game(nextId++, userId, word);
        games.push(newGame);
        return newGame;
    }

    module.exports.get =
        (id) => games.find(game => game.id === parseInt(id, 10));
```

Now let's go through our application from the top down. In our index view
(views/index.hjs), we'll add simple a HTML form for creating a new game.

```
    <body>
      <h1>{{ title }}</h1>
      <form action="/games" method="POST">
        <input type="text" name="word"
               placeholder="Enter a word to guess..." />
        <input type="submit" />
      </form>
    <body>
```

When submitted, this form will make a POST request to /games. At the moment, this
would return a 404 error since we have nothing mounted at that route (you can try
this in a browser it if you like). We can add a new games route to handle this request.
We add the following code under routes/games.js:

```
    'use strict';

    const express = require('express');
    const router = express.Router();
    const service = require('../services/games');

    router.post('/', function(req, res, next) {
        const word = req.body.word;
        if (word && /^[A-Za-z]{3,}$/.test(word)) {
            service.create(req.user.id, word);
            res.redirect('/');
        } else {
```

```
        res.status(400).send('Word must be at least three characters
long and contain only letters');
    }
});

module.exports = router;
```

There is quite a lot going on in our new routing middleware:

- `router.post` creates a handler for an HTTP POST request.
- `req.body` contains form values, thanks to the `bodyParser` middleware in `app.js`.
- `req.user.id` contains the current user, thanks to our users middleware.
- `res.redirect()` issues a redirect to reload the page. It is important to always issue a redirect after a successful POST request. This avoids duplicate form submissions.
- `res.status()` sets an alternative HTTP status code for the response, in this case a 400 for a validation failure.

Our route looks for a field named word in the request body. It then checks this field is defined and not empty (both undefined and the empty string are *falsey* in JavaScript, so they behave as false in conditional tests). It also checks that the field matches a regular expression specifying our validity rule.

Finally, the route makes use of our service module to actually create the new game. It is common practice for routing middleware to delegate application logic to other modules. Its main responsibility is to define the HTTP interface of the application. Other modules are responsible for implementing the actual application logic. In this way, our routes and middleware are comparable to controllers in MVC frameworks.

We also need to mount this route at the /games path. The following code is from app.js:

```
var routes = require('./routes/index');
var games = require('./routes/games');
...
app.use('/', routes);
app.use('/games', games);
```

# Communicating via Ajax

Having created a game, we need a way of playing it. Since the whole point of a guessing game is that the word is secret, we don't want to send the whole word to the client. Instead, we just want to let clients know the length of the word and provide a way for them to verify their guesses.

To do this, we'll first need to expand our games service module:

```
class Game {
    constructor(id, setBy, word) {
        this.id = id;
        this.setBy = setBy;
        this.word = word.toUpperCase();
    }

    positionsOf(character) {
        let positions = [];
        for (let i in this.word) {
            if (this.word[i] === character.toUpperCase()) {
                positions.push(i);
            }
        }
        return positions;
    }
}
```

Now we can add two new routes to our games route:

```
const checkGameExists = function(id, res, callback) {
    const game = service.get(id);
    if (game) {
        callback(game);
    } else {
        res.status(404).send('Non-existent game ID');
    }
}

router.get('/:id', function(req, res, next) {
    checkGameExists(
        req.params.id,
        res,
        game => res.render('game', {
            length: game.word.length,
            id: game.id
```

```
        }));
    });

    router.post('/:id/guesses', function(req, res, next) {
        checkGameExists(
            req.params.id,
            res,
            game => {
                res.send({
                    positions: game.positionsOf(req.body.letter)
                });
            }
        );
    });
```

These two routes make use of a shared function for retrieving the game and returning a 404 status code if it does not exist. The GET handler renders a view, as with our index route. The POST handler calls `res.send()`, passing in a JavaScript object. Express will automatically turn this into a JSON response to the client. This makes it very easy to build JSON-based APIs in express.

We'll now create a view and client-side script for communicating with this API. We add the following code under `views/game.hjs`:

```
<!DOCTYPE html>
<html>
  <head>
    <title>Hangman - Game #{{id}}</title>
    <link rel="stylesheet" href="/stylesheets/style.css" />
    <script src="https://cdnjs.cloudflare.com/ajax/libs/jquery/2.2.3/jquery.min.js"></script>
    <script src="/scripts/game.js"></script>
    <base href="/games/{{ id }}/">
  </head>
  <body>
    <h1>Hangman - Game #{{id}}</h1>
    <h2 id="word" data-length="{{ length }}"></h2>
    <p>Press letter keys to guess</p>
    <h3>Missed letters:</h3>
    <p id="missedLetters"></p>
  </body>
</html>
```

We add the following code under `public/scripts/game.js`:

```javascript
$(function() {
    'use strict';

    var word = $('#word');
    var length = word.data('length');

    // Create placeholders for each letter
    for (var i = 0; i < length; ++i) {
        word.append('<span>_</span>');
    }

    var guessedLetters = [];
    var guessLetter = function(letter) {
        $.post('guesses', { letter: letter })
            .done(function(data) {
                if (data.positions.length) {
                    data.positions.forEach(function(position) {
                        word.find('span').eq(position).text(letter);
                    });
                } else {
                    $('#missedLetters')
                        .append('<span>' + letter + '</span>');
                }
            });
    }

    $(document).keydown(function(event) {
        // Letter keys have key codes in the range 65-90
        if (event.which >= 65 && event.which <= 90) {
            var letter = String.fromCharCode(event.which);
            if (guessedLetters.indexOf(letter) === -1) {
                guessedLetters.push(letter);
                guessLetter(letter);
            }
        }
    });
});
```

Note that in the client-side script we drop back to the ECMAScript 5 standard (for example, `var` instead of `let`, and no arrow function). This ensures the widest possible compatibility. The latest versions of all mainstream browsers would support the elements of ES2015 syntax that we've been using so far though.

Also note that we don't have Node.js modules available on the client side. We fall back to wrapping our code in a function to isolate the scope. We'll look at ways to make client-side code more modular in a later chapter.

Our client-side script uses jQuery. We won't go into detail on client-side frameworks, but it's worth quickly explaining the features used here. The jQuery library provides a consistent API for DOM manipulation that works across all browsers, as well as a number of useful tools for client-side functionality.

The main jQuery API is available through the `$` object, which is a function. The first thing our script does is call `$` and pass it a callback, which jQuery will execute once the page has finished loading. Our other calls to `$` pass in a string or a DOM element. Strings are interpreted as a CSS selector for choosing elements. In both cases, `$` returns a wrapper around a set of DOM elements with some useful methods, for example:

- The `data` method allows us to read the elements' `data-` attributes
- The `append` method allows us to add new child elements
- Methods such as `keydown` allow us to bind handler functions for events

There are also some utility methods defined on the `$` object itself. These are more like static methods and don't relate to a specific DOM element. The `post()` method is an example of this.

Our script uses jQuery's `post()` method to issue an Ajax POST request. This returns an object with a `done()` method, to which we can pass a callback to be executed when the request completes. Here, we can make use of the JSON data returned by our API. In this case, we fill in any positions that match our guessed letter.

If we run the application at this point, we have a (very) minimal working game. First, visit `http://localhost:3000/` and create a new game by submitting a valid word. Then visit `http://localhost:3000/games/1` to play. It should look something like the following:

# Implementing other data operations

So far, we have seen how to create or retrieve a single game, or submit a single guess for a game. Applications also commonly need to list data or delete entries. The principles here are much the same as we've seen already. But to implement these operations, we'll need some new syntax.

# Listing data in views

Let's first allow users to see a list of games they've created or that have been created by others. Our chosen view engine, Hogan, is based on Mustache, which has a very simple syntax for displaying lists. We can add these two lists to our `index.hjs` view, as follows:

```
<h2>Games created by you</h2>
<ul id="createdGames">
  {{#createdGames}}
    <li>{{word}}</li>
  {{/createdGames}}
</ul>
```

```
<h2>Games available to play</h2>
<ul id="availableGames">
  {{#availableGames}}
    <li><a href="/games/{{id}}">#{{id}}</a></li>
  {{/availableGames}}
</ul>
```

In order to populate these lists, we'll need a couple of new methods in our `games.js` service module:

```
module.exports.createdBy =
  (userId) => games.filter(game => game.setBy === userId);

module.exports.availableTo =
  (userId) => games.filter(game => game.setBy !== userId);
```

Finally, we'll need to expose these to our index view from our route:

```
var express = require('express');
var router = express.Router();
var games = require('../services/games');

router.get('/', function(req, res, next) {
  res.render('index', {
    title: 'Hangman',
    userId: req.user.id,
    createdGames: games.createdBy(req.user.id),
    availableGames: games.availableTo(req.user.id)
  });
});

module.exports = router;
```

Now, our index page shows games created by the current user and provides convenient links to games created by others. You can experiment with this functionality by using two separate browser sessions again to visit `http://localhost:3000`. The result should look something like the following:

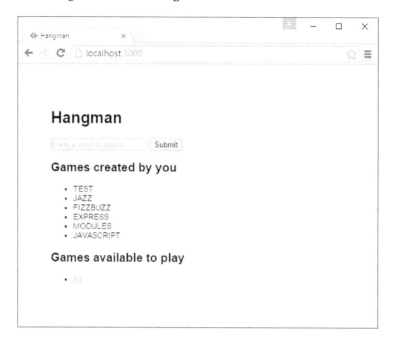

# Issuing a delete request from the client

To allow users to remove games that they have created, we'll first need to add a method to our Game class:

```
class Game {
    constructor(id, setBy, word) {
        this.id = id;
        this.setBy = setBy;
        this.word = word.toUpperCase();
    }

    positionsOf(character) {
        let positions = [];
        for (let i in this.word) {
            if (this.word[i] === character.toUpperCase()) {
                positions.push(i);
            }
        }
    }
```

```
        return positions;
    }

    remove() {
        games.splice(games.indexOf(this), 1);
    }
}
```

Next we can create a new handler for `delete` requests in our games route:

```
router.delete('/:id', function(req, res, next) {
    checkGameExists(
        req.params.id,
        res,
        game => {
            if (game.setBy === req.user.id) {
                game.remove();
                res.send();
            } else {
                res.status(403).send(
                    'You don't have permission to delete this game'
                );
            }
        }
    );
});
```

Finally, we can make use of this from the client. The following code is from `views/index.hjs`:

```
    <head>
      <title>{{ title }}</title>
      <link rel="stylesheet" href="/stylesheets/style.css" />
      <script src="https://cdnjs.cloudflare.com/ajax/libs/jquery/2.2.3/
    jquery.min.js"></script>
      <script src="/scripts/index.js"></script>
    </head>

    ...

      {{#createdGames}}
        <li class="game">
          {{word}}
          <a class="delete" href="/games/{{id}}">(delete)</a>
        </li>
      {{/createdGames}}
```

We add the following code under `public/scripts/index.js`:

```
$(function() {
    'use strict';

    $('#createdGames').on('click', '.delete', function() {
        var $this = $(this);
        $.ajax($this.attr('href'), {
            method: 'delete'
        }).done(function() {
            $this.closest('.game').remove();
        });
        event.preventDefault();
    });
});
```

Note that, unlike GET and POST, jQuery has no convenience function for `delete` requests. So we drop back to the lower level `.ajax()` function and specify the HTTP method explicitly.

If you visit the application in a browser and create a new game again, you should now see a link to delete the game.

# Splitting up Express views using partials

Deleting a game does not cause the page to refresh, but creating a new game does. We can fix this by creating games via an Ajax call, consistent with how we delete games. In order for this to work, the client-side script that handles the call needs to know which HTML to add to the page when a new game is created.

We could repeat the HTML structure of the view within the client-side JavaScript. However, it would be better for the server to return the correct HTML fragment, and to reuse the same template for this as it uses it to render the list on the page initially.

We can do this by splitting the HTML structure for a game within the list into a partial view. This is a view template for an HTML fragment rather than a complete page. We add the following code under `views/createdGame.hjs`:

```
<li class="game">
  {{word}}
  <a class="delete" href="/games/{{id}}">(delete)</a>
</li>
```

With the view engine that we're using (Hogan), we need to let views know about available partials when rendering them (other view engines allow partials to be resolved automatically). The following code is from `routes/index.js`:

```
res.render('index', {
  title: 'Hangman',
  userId: req.user.id,
  createdGames: games.createdBy(req.user.id),
  availableGames: games.availableTo(req.user.id),
  partials: { createdGame: 'createdGame' }
});
```

We can use the partial within our main view as follows. We'll also add IDs to our HTML elements, which we will reference from our client-side JavaScript shortly. The following code is from `views/index.hjs`:

```
<form action="/games" method="POST" id="createGame">
  <input type="text" name="word" id="word"
         placeholder="Enter a word to guess..." />
  <input type="submit" />    </form>
<h2>Games created by you</h2>
<ul id="createdGames">
  {{#createdGames}}
    {{> createdGame}}
  {{/createdGames}}
</ul>
```

Now we can update our games route to return only this fragment to the client when creating a new game. The following code is from `routes/games.js`:

```
router.post('/', function(req, res, next) {
    let word = req.body.word;
    if (word && /^[A-Za-z]{3,}$/.test(word)) {
        const game = service.create(req.user.id, word);
        res.redirect(`/games/${game.id}/created`);
    } else {
        ...
    }
});
...
router.get('/:id/created', function(req, res, next) {
    checkGameExists(
        req.params.id,
        res,
        game => res.render('createdGame', game));
});
```

Finally, we can make use of this in our client-side script. The following code is from `public/scripts/index.js`:

```
$(function() {
  'use strict';
  $('#createGame').submit(function(event) {
    $.post($(this).attr('action'), { word: $('#word').val() },
      function(result) {
        $('#createdGames').append(result);
      });
    event.preventDefault();
  });
  ...
});
```

# Summary

In this chapter, we have started building out our own application by creating new middleware and service modules. We've read user-submitted data from forms and acted on it. We've implemented a JSON API on the server side and communicated with this from the client using Ajax. We've used partial views to render common components.

So far, we've seen how to write JavaScript code and implement various functionality in Node.js. This is good for prototyping, but isn't enough for a maintainable project. It's also important to write automated tests for our code, which is the subject of the next chapter.

# Testing Node.js Applications

**6**

So far, we have only been testing our code by exercising it manually. This isn't a very sustainable approach as our application becomes larger. Ideally, we should regularly exercise all the functionality of our application to check for regressions. This would quickly become prohibitively time-consuming if we continued to use only manual testing. It is much more effective to maintain a suite of automated tests. These also bring many other benefits, for example, acting as documentation of our code for other developers.

In this chapter, we will cover the following topics:

- Writing automated unit tests for our application
- Introducing new libraries to help us write more descriptive tests
- Seeing how to create and use test doubles in JavaScript
- Exercising our application's web interface using HTTP client tests
- Adding full-stack integration tests using browser automation
- Establishing a structure for writing further tests as we expand our codebase

## Writing a simple test in Node.js

Node.js comes with a built-in module called `assert` that can be used for testing. We can use it to write a simple test for the games service that we wrote in *Chapter 5, Building Dynamic Websites*. We add the following code under `gameServiceTest.js`:

```
'use strict';

let assert = require('assert');
let service = require('./services/games.js')

// Given
```

```
service.create('firstUserId', 'testing');

// When
let games = service.availableTo('secondUserId');

// Then
assert.equal(games.length, 1);
let game = games[0];
assert.equal(game.setBy, 'firstUserId');
assert.equal(game.word, 'TESTING');
```

Note that the `assert.equal` function takes the actual value as the first argument and the expected value as the second argument. This is the opposite way around to JUnit's built-in `Assert.Equals`, and the classic-style `Assert.AreEqual` in NUnit. It's important to get these parameters the right way around so that they appear correctly in error messages when an assertion fails.

**Given, When, Then**

The *Given*, *When*, and *Then* comments in the preceding test are not specific to JavaScript or any of the test frameworks we'll be using, but are generally a good tool for structuring tests to keep them focused and readable.

We can now verify our code using the following command:

```
> node gameServiceTest.js
> echo %errorlevel%
```

An exit code of 0 indicates that our test completed successfully without any errors. Although we haven't been following test-driven development (writing a failing test first before adding any new code), it's still important to see each test fail to confirm that it's testing something. Try altering the `availableTo` function in `services/games.js` to return an empty array, and run the test again.

Not only do we now get a non-zero exit code, but we also get an error containing our assertion failure. Our test output still isn't particular compelling, though. Also, the lack of structure in our test script will make it harder to navigate as we add more tests. We can address both of these issues by making use of one of the testing libraries available for JavaScript.

# Structuring the codebase for tests

As we write more tests for our application, we'll benefit from having more structure to our tests. It's common to have at least one test file per production module. It will also be useful to have a way of running all of our tests and seeing the overall result.

We're going to start adding tests under a `test` directory. From this point on in the book, we're also going to keep all of our application code under a `src` directory. This will make it easier to navigate our codebase and to keep production and test code separate.

If you're following along with the book at this point, you should move `app.js` and all the folders (apart from the `bin` folder) under a new `src` directory, and update the startup script as follows in `bin/www`:

```
var app = require('../src/app');
var debug = require('debug')('hangman:server');
var http = require('http');
```

# Writing BDD-style tests with Mocha

From C# or Java, you may be most familiar with the xUnit-style of tests used by NUnit, JUnit, and so on. This style structures tests into classes, and turns method names into test names. This can be a bit restrictive, and isn't common in JavaScript testing. JavaScript test frameworks make use of the less structured, and more dynamic, nature of the language to allow more flexibility.

There are several different styles for writing tests in JavaScript. The most common is the so-called **behavior-driven development** (BDD) style in which we describe the behavior of our application in plain English. This is the default style of the most popular JavaScript testing frameworks. It is also common in frameworks for other programming platforms, most notably RSpec for Ruby.

We'll be using a popular test framework named Mocha. Let's first add this to our application:

```
> npm install mocha --save-dev
```

Note that `--save-dev` adds Mocha to our `package.json` file as a **development dependency**. This indicates that it's not needed in our production code, and npm doesn't need to install it in production environments. We'll also update this file to let npm run our tests using Mocha, by adding a test script as follows:

```
"scripts": {
  "start": "node ./bin/www",
  "test": "node node_modules/mocha/bin/mocha test/**/*.js"
},
```

This tells npm to execute scripts under the `/test/` directory as tests using Mocha when we run npm `test` from the command line.

**Mocha and Jasmine**

There are a large number of different testing frameworks available for JavaScript. The most well-established are Jasmine and Mocha. They have comparable features and both support the same syntax for writing tests. They are both well-documented, and switching between the two is easy.

Jasmine was originally aimed more at testing client-side JavaScript in the browser. Mocha was originally more focused on testing server-side Node.js code.

Nowadays, both frameworks are well-suited for either environment. Jasmine also has more *batteries included*, which can make it quicker to get started with. Mocha delegates more features to other libraries, giving the user more choice about how they prefer to write tests.

Now we just need to add some tests! Mocha provides global functions named `describe` and `it` for structuring our tests. These functions each take two arguments: a string describing the behavior of our application and a callback defining the tests for that behavior. The following code snippet shows our previous test rewritten using Mocha. We add the following code under `test/services/games.js`:

```
'use strict';

const assert = require('assert');
const service = require('../../src/services/games.js');

describe('Game service', () => {
    const firstUserId = 'user-id-1';
    const secondUserId = 'user-id-2';
```

```
describe('list of available games', () => {
    it('should include games set by other users', () => {
        // Given
        service.create(firstUserId, 'testing');

        // When
        const games = service.availableTo(secondUserId);

        // Then
        assert.equal(games.length, 1);
        const game = games[0];
        assert.equal(game.setBy, firstUserId);
        assert.equal(game.word, 'TESTING');
    });
});
});
```

Now try running the previous test using `npm test`. You should see output like the following (the exact appearance will depend on what console you are using):

```
Game service
    list of available games
        √ should include games set by other users


1 passing (8ms)
```

Note how we get a much more descriptive output of our tests. Also note the use of nested describe callbacks in our test to build up a description of our application. The benefit of this becomes clearer as we add more tests. Try adding the following test after the first test:

```
it('should not include games set by the same user', () => {
    // Given
    service.create(firstUserId, 'first');
    service.create(secondUserId, 'second');

    // When
    const games = service.availableTo(secondUserId);

    // Then
    assert.equal(games.length, 1);
    const game = games[0];
    assert.notEqual(game.setBy, secondUserId);
});
```

Run the tests again using `npm test`. This time, we get a test failure from Mocha:

```
Game service
  list of available games
    √ should include games set by other users
    1) should not include games set by the same user


1 passing (10ms)
1 failing

1) Game service list of available games should not include
games set by the same user:

   AssertionError: 2 == 1
   + expected - actual


   -2
   +1
```

# Resetting state between tests

Our second test fails because it retrieves two games from the service. But this is not because our production code is failing to filter games correctly. In fact, there are two games created by the first user. One of these has been carried over from the previous test.

It's important for tests to be independent and isolated from each other. To this end, we need to clean up any state between tests. In this case, we want to delete all the games we created. The games service doesn't give us a method for clearing all games. We can only remove individual games after retrieving them. There are a few options available to us here:

- We could keep track of all the games we create during each test and delete them all at the end. This might seem the most obvious solution, but it's a bit fragile. It would be easy to miss a single game that might cause confusing test failures later.

- We could rewrite the games service module to export a function for creating a new service, and instantiate a new service for each test. In general, it's a good idea to try and isolate tests by creating fresh objects under each test. However, this is only useful if the object doesn't store any external state. We may well want to change the implementation of the games service later, to store data externally in a persistent datastore.

- We could add a clear method to the games service to wipe out all its data. It's not wrong to create methods like this for the purposes of supporting tests. However, it's preferable to interact with the application via its existing API if possible.

The games service does offer a way of retrieving all current games. We just need to pass in a user ID that doesn't match the setter of any game. We can then go through and delete all games. We want to do this before every test, which we can do using Mocha's `beforeEach` hook:

```
describe('Game service', () => {
    const firstUserId = 'user-id-1';
    const secondUserId = 'user-id-2';

    beforeEach(() => {
        let gamesCreated = service.availableTo("not-a-user");
        gamesCreated.forEach(game => game.remove());
    });

    describe('list of available games', () => {
```

If we re-run our tests, they now both pass correctly. There is also an `afterEach` hook in Mocha, which we could have used instead. This would have worked, but it's safer for tests to defend themselves by cleaning up first, rather than relying on other tests to clean up after themselves.

# Using Chai for assertions

Another way to make our tests more descriptive is how we write our assertions. Although the built-in Node.js assert module has been useful so far, it is a bit limited. It only contains a small number of simple methods for basic assertions.

You may have experience of Fluent Assertions or NUnit's Constraint model in .NET, or AssertJ in Java. Compared to these, the Node.js assert module might seem quite primitive.

There are several assertion frameworks available for JavaScript. We'll be using Chai (`http://chaijs.com`), which supports three different styles for writing assertions. The `assert` style follows the traditional xUnit assertions, as in JUnit, or the classic model of NUnit. The `should` and `expect` styles provide a natural language interface for building more descriptive assertions.

Any of these styles is a perfectly valid choice for writing test assertions. The important thing is to pick a style for your codebase and use it consistently. We will be using Chai's expect syntax throughout this book. This is one of the more common styles in JavaScript testing. The Jasmine test framework has built-in assertions that follow a similar style.

Let's first install Chai by running the following on the command line:

```
> npm install chai --save-dev
```

Then update our tests to use it:

```
const expect = require('chai').expect;
const service = require('../../src/services/games.js');

...

    it('should include games created by other users', () => {
        // Given
        service.create(firstUserId, 'testing');

        // When
        const games = service.availableTo(secondUserId);

        // Then
        expect(games.length).to.equal(1);
        const game = games[0];
        expect(game.setBy).to.equal(firstUserId);
        expect(game.word).to.equal('TESTING');
    });

    it('should not include games created by the same user', () => {
        // Given
        service.create(firstUserId, 'first');
        service.create(secondUserId, 'second');

        // When
        const games = service.availableTo(secondUserId);

        // Then
        expect(games.length).to.equal(1);
        let game = games[0];
        expect(game.setBy).not.to.equal(secondUserId);
    });
```

The change isn't particularly dramatic at this point as we're only making simple assertions. But the natural language interface will allow us to specify more detailed assertions in a descriptive way.

# Creating test doubles

There are more tests we could write for the games service, but let's look at a different module for now. How would we go about testing our `users` middleware? The following code is from `middleware/users.js`:

```
module.exports = function(req, res, next) {
    let userId = req.cookies.userId;
    if (!userId) {
        userId = uuid.v4();
        res.cookie('userId', userId);
    }
    req.user = {
        id: userId
    };
    next();
};
```

In order to test this class, we will need to pass in arguments for the `req`, `res`, and `next` parameters with which our code interacts. We don't have a real request, response, or middleware pipeline available, so we need to create some stand-in values instead. Stand-in values such as this are generally called **test doubles**. Our code reads an attribute from the request and calls the cookie method on the response. We can create test doubles for these as follows, in a new test script under `test/middleware/users.js`:

```
'use strict';

const middleware = require('../../middleware/users.js');
const expect = require('chai').expect;

describe('Users middleware', () => {
    const defaultUserId = 'user-id-1';
    let request, response;

    beforeEach(() => {
        request = { cookies: {} };
        response = { cookie: () => {} };
    });
```

```
        it('if the user already signed in, reads their ID from a cookie
and exposes the user on the request', () => {
            // Given
            request.cookies.userId = defaultUserId;

            // When
            middleware(request, response, () => {});

            // Then
            expect(request.user).to.exist;
            expect(request.user.id).to.equal(defaultUserId);
        });
    });
```

Here, we simply create a plain JavaScript object to represent the request. This allows us to verify that the production code reads from, and writes to, the request properties correctly. We just pass in the minimum possible input for the response object and the `next` function to allow the code to execute. This is very easy to do in JavaScript, partly because it is not statically typed. Creating test doubles like this in C# or Java can be a lot more work as the compiler will insist on the test doubles matching the corresponding parameter types.

We also need to test that our middleware calls the next middleware in the chain, as this is important behavior. This is slightly more complex than just creating an object with simple properties. We can still create a suitable test double by defining a new function that records when it is called (this kind of test double is called a **spy**):

```
    it('calls the next middleware in the chain', () => {
        // Given
        let calledNext = false;
        const next = () => calledNext = true;

        // When
        middleware(request, response, next);

        // Then
        expect(calledNext).to.be.true;
    });
```

This works perfectly well, but will become more cumbersome if we want to test more complex calls, for example, if we want to check for multiple calls or make further assertions about the arguments passed in. We can simplify this by making use of a framework to create test doubles for us.

# Creating test doubles using Sinon.JS

Sinon.JS is a framework for creating all kinds of test doubles. Let's first install it into our application by running the following on the command line:

```
> npm install sinon --save-dev
```

Now let's simplify our previous test and write a more complex test using test doubles created by Sinon.JS:

```
const expect = require('chai').expect;
const sinon = require('sinon');

...

    it('calls the next middleware in the chain', () => {
        // Given
        const next = sinon.spy();

        // When
        middleware(request, {}, next);

        // Then
        expect(next.called).to.be.true;
    });

    it('if the user is not already signed in, ' +
        'creates a new user id and stores it in a cookie', () => {
        // Given
        request.cookies.userId = undefined;
        response = { cookie: sinon.spy() };

        // When
        middleware(request, response, () => {});

        // Then
        expect(request.user).to.exist;
        const newUserId = request.user.id;
        expect(newUserId).to.exist;
        expect(response.cookie.calledWith(
            'userId', newUserId)).to.be.true;
    });
```

Sinon.JS spies keep track of the details of all calls made to them and provide a convenient API for checking these. This allows us to keep our test code simple and readable. There are many more properties than just the `called` and `calledWith` user here. Take a look at the Sinon.JS documentation at `http://sinonjs.org/docs/#spies-api` to see some of the other ways we can verify the calls made against a spy.

**Spies, stubs, and mocks**

If you read more of the Sinon.JS documentation, you'll see that it's very explicit about the difference between spies, stubs, and mocks. This is in contrast to most popular test double frameworks in Java and .NET, which tend to call all test doubles by the same name (typically mock or fake). In reality though, most instances of test doubles typically only act as a spy (used for verifying side-effects) or a stub (used for providing data, or throwing exceptions to test error-handling). A true mock verifies a specific sequence of calls and returns specific data to the code under test. Although some of the early mocking frameworks in Java and .NET only supported this type of test double (now sometimes called a *strict mock*), it isn't common practice anymore. This is because it quite tightly couples test and production code and makes refactoring more difficult. It's especially rare to have more than one mock (as opposed to just a stub or spy) in a single test.

# Testing an Express application

While using Sinon.JS makes our tests neater, they still depend on the details of the Express middleware API and how we're using it. This might be appropriate for our middleware module as we want to ensure that it fulfills a particular contract (especially calling `next` and setting `request.user`). For most middleware, though, especially our routes, this approach would couple our tests too closely to our implementation.

It would be better to test the actual behavior of each route by making HTTP requests to it and examining the responses, rather than checking for specific low-level interactions with the request and response objects. This gives us more flexibility to change our implementation and refactor our code, without needing to change the tests. Thus, our tests can support this process (by catching regressions) rather than hindering it (by having to be updated to match our implementation).

On other platforms, testing a whole application can be quite a heavyweight process. It is possible to start up a server in process, for example, using Jetty in Java or Katana in .NET. Newer application frameworks, such as Spring Boot or NancyFx, also make this process easier. These are still likely to be relatively slow and resource-intensive tests, though.

In Node.js, starting up an application server is easy and very lightweight. We just use the same `http.createServer` call as we've seen before, and pass it an application. To test our route in isolation, we'll bootstrap a new application containing just this route. Let's see how we can use this to test the delete endpoint of our games route. We add the following code under `test/routes/games.js`:

```
'use strict';

const http = require('http');
const express = require('express');
const bodyParser = require('body-parser');
const expect = require('chai').expect;
const gamesService = require('../../src/services/games.js');

const TEST_PORT = 5000, userId = 'test-user-id';

describe('/games', () => {
  let server;
  const makeRequest = (method, path, callback) => {
    http.request({
      method: method,
      port: TEST_PORT,
      path: path
    }, callback).end();
  };

  before(done => {
    const app = express();
    app.use(bodyParser.json());
    app.use((req, res, next) => {
      req.user = { id: userId }; next();
    });

    const games = require('../../src/routes/games.js');
    app.use('/games', games);

    server = http.createServer(app).listen(TEST_PORT, done);
```

```
    });

    afterEach(() => {
      const gamesCreated = gamesService.availableTo("non-user");
      gamesCreated.forEach(game => game.remove());
    });

    after(done => {
      server.close(done);
    });

    describe('/:id DELETE', () => {
      it('should allow users to delete their own games', done => {
        const game = gamesService.create(userId, 'test');

        makeRequest('DELETE', '/games/' + game.id, response => {
          expect(response.statusCode).to.equal(200);
          expect(gamesService.createdBy(userId)).to.be.empty;
          done();
        });
      });
    });
  });
});
```

This might seem like quite a lot of code, but remember that we're firing up an entire application here. Also, most of this code will be reused for multiple tests. Let's work through what it does.

The `before` callback creates our server, just as we saw in *Chapter 2, Getting Started with Node.js*, listening on a special port for use by our tests. It also sets up some stub middleware to simulate a current user on the request. The `afterEach` callback clears up any created games (as we saw before in the test of the games service). Note that since we're running in the same process, we can trivially interact with the same data layer that our application is using. Finally, the `after` function asks the server to stop listening for connections.

The test itself is very simple: we just create a game set by the current user (as in our service tests before) and then issue a request to delete it. This makes use of our own `makeRequest` function, which simply calls through to Node's `http.request`. We can then inspect the response object to check for the appropriate status code, and check the service for the desired effect.

**Writing asynchronous tests in Mocha**

Notice that our test and all of the callbacks to Mocha's hook functions discussed above (except for afterEach) take a done parameter. This is because all of these tests perform some asynchronous work. Mocha makes it very easy to write asynchronous tests or hooks: you just make your callback function take a single parameter (called done by convention), and call it when processing is complete. If it's not called within a timeout (which defaults to 2 seconds but can be changed), then Mocha fails the test.

Let's run our tests again using the `npm test` command. Notice that all of the tests still finish very quickly (tens of milliseconds on my machine), even though we're starting up our whole server-side application. You may also notice the output is a bit messy due to log output from the server. We can easily suppress this by updating app.js as follows:

```
//app.use(favicon(path.join(__dirname, 'public', 'favicon.ico')));
if (app.get('env') === 'development') {
    app.use(logger('dev'));
}
app.use(bodyParser.json());
```

The `'env'` property of an Express application comes from the NODE_ENV environment variable (or defaults to development if this is not present). This is useful for differentiating between production and development environments. Since it defaults to `development`, we also need to set it to something else in order to suppress this logging in our tests. We can do this by updating our test script in `package.json` as follows:

```
"scripts": {
  "start": "node ./bin/www",
  "test": "set NODE_ENV=test && node node_modules/mocha/bin/mocha
test/**/*.js"
},
```

# Simplifying tests using SuperAgent

While our tests are fast, and setting up the server is quite straightforward, we do have quite a lot of code for making requests to the server and handling responses. This would become more complex if we needed to make a wider variety of requests, or were interested in more than just the response status code or headers.

We can simplify our tests by using a library that provides a simpler API for communicating with the server. SuperAgent (https://visionmedia.github.io/superagent/) is a JavaScript library that provides a fluent, readable syntax for making HTTP requests. This can be used for Ajax requests in the browser, or for requests in a Node.js application as we're doing here.

We'll make use of SuperAgent through a lightweight wrapper called SuperTest (https://github.com/visionmedia/supertest), which makes testing Node.js-based HTTP applications even more convenient.

First, we add SuperTest into our application using npm, by running the following on the command line:

```
> npm install supertest --save-dev
```

Now we can rewrite our tests as follows:

```
'use strict';

const express = require('express');
const bodyParser = require('body-parser');
const request = require('supertest');
const expect = require('chai').expect;
const gamesService = require('../../src/services/games.js');

const userId = 'test-user-id';

describe('/games', () => {
  let agent, app;

  before(() => {
    app = express();
    app.use(bodyParser.json());
    app.use((req, res, next) => {
      req.user = { id: userId }; next();
    });

    const games = require('../../src/routes/games.js');
    app.use('/games', games);
  });

  beforeEach(() => {
    agent = request.agent(app);
  });
```

```
describe('/:id DELETE', () => {
    it('should allow users to delete their own games', done => {
        const game = gamesService.create(userId, 'test');

        agent
          .delete('/games/' + game.id)
          .expect(200)
          .expect(() =>
              expect(gamesService.createdBy(userId)).to.be.empty)
          .end(done);
    });
  });
});
```

SuperTest and SuperAgent take care of starting up the server for our application, and provide a much simpler API for making requests. Note the use of a request **agent**, which represents a single browser session.

SuperAgent provides a number of functions (get, post, delete, and so on) for making HTTP requests. These can be chained with calls to the expect function (not to be confused with Chai's expect) to verify properties of the response, such as the status code. We can also pass in a callback to make specific checks about the response, or verify side-effects (as we do in the previous example).

Note that it is important to always call the end function to make sure any expectation errors are thrown and fail the test. We can pass Mocha's done callback to end the test when the request is completed.

Now that we've simplified our test code, we can easily add more tests for our routes. For example, let's add some tests to cover the negative cases of our delete endpoint:

```
it('should not allow users to delete games that they did not set',
done => {
    const game = gamesService.create('another-user-id', 'test');
    agent
      .delete('/games/' + game.id)
      .expect(403)
      .expect(() => expect(gamesService.get(game.id).ok))
      .end(done);
});

it('should return a 404 for requests to delete a game that no
longer exists', done => {
    const game = gamesService.create(userId, 'test');
    agent
      .delete(`/games/${game.id}`)
```

```
    .expect(200)
    .end(function(err) {
      if (err) {
        done(err);
      } else {
        agent
          .delete('/games/' + game.id)
          .expect(404, done);
      }
    });
  });
```

# Full-stack testing with PhantomJS

We have now written unit tests for logic at the core of our application and integration tests for our server-side routes. We don't yet have any automated tests that cover our views and client-side scripts as our manual testing throughout the previous chapters did.

We can write unit tests for client-side scripts using Mocha. However, all of our current client-side scripts interact with the server, so aren't good candidates for unit testing. Our manual tests are really full-stack tests of our whole application, including the interaction between the server and the client.

In order to achieve this in an automated test, we will need to use some form of browser automation. **PhantomJS** is a headless browser with a JavaScript API that allows us to automate it directly. We can write a simple test for our game page using this.

First, we'll install PhantomJS within our project by running the following on the command line:

```
> npm install phantomjs-prebuilt --save-dev
```

 PhantomJS is not a Node.js module. It is a standalone, headless web browser. The npm module is just a convenient way of installing it and making it a dependency of the project. PhantomJS cannot be invoked from Node.js, except to execute it as a separate child process.

Now we can implement a test as follows, under `integration-test/game.js`:

```
(function() {
    'use strict';

    var expect = require('chai').expect;
```

```
var page = require('webpage').create();
var rootUrl = 'http://localhost:3000';

withGame('Example', function() {
    expect(getText('#word')).to.equal('_____');

    page.evaluate(function() {
        $(document).ajaxComplete(window.callPhantom);
    });

    page.sendEvent('keydown', page.event.key.E);
    page.onCallback = verify(function() {
        expect(getText('#word')).to.equal('E_____E');
        expect(getText('#missedLetters')).to.be.empty;

        page.sendEvent('keydown', page.event.key.T);
        page.onCallback = verify(function() {
            expect(getText('#word')).to.equal('E_____E');
            expect(getText('#missedLetters')).to.equal('T');

            console.log('Test completed successfully!');
            phantom.exit();
        });
    });
});

function withGame(word, callback) {
    ...
}

function getText(selector) {
    return page.evaluate(function(s) {
        return $(s).text();
    }, selector);
}

function verify(expectations) {
    return function() {
        try {
            expectations();
        } catch(e) {
            console.log('Test failed!');
            handleError(e.message);
        }
```

```
            }
        }

        function handleError(message) {
            console.log(message);
            phantom.exit(1);
        }

        phantom.onError = page.onError = handleError;
    }());
```

Make sure the application is running (using `npm start`), then execute the test by running the following on the command line:

```
> node node_modules/phantomjs-prebuilt/bin/phantomjs integration-test/
game.js
```

Let's take a look through the code to understand how it works. Note that we're running in the browser environment here rather than Node.js, so fall back to the ECMAScript 5 syntax (for example, `var` instead of `let`, and no arrow functions).

The omitted `withGame` method (which you can find in the book's companion code) uses PhantomJS to load the index view and submit a new game, then clears PhantomJS's cookies and opens the game as a new user, before invoking the callback passed to `withGame`.

In our test, we create a game to guess the word *example*, then invoke JavaScript within the page to make assertions about its contents. The `getText` function uses PhantomJS's `page.evaluate` function to run some JavaScript within the context of the page, and return a value. Note that the callback function passed to `page.evaluate` does not have access to the wider execution context of our script. We can, however, specify additional arguments to the `page.evaluate` call, which is how we pass in the selector for jQuery.

We then use `page.evaluate` again to set up a callback each time an Ajax request completes. Here, we use `window.callPhantom`, which executes within the context of the page, and triggers `page.onCallback`, which executes within the context of our test.

Finally, we use `page.sendEvent` to trigger a keyboard event in the browser. Note that this is not the same as using pure JavaScript within the browser to trigger a DOM event, but is an instruction directly to PhantomJS to simulate the `keypress` event as if it had come from the user.

If we put all this together, we get the following:

- We use `page.sendEvent` to simulate pressing a keyboard key
- This causes our production code to send off an Ajax request
- When this request completes, `window.callPhantom` is invoked in the context of the browser
- This causes PhantomJS to invoke our `page.onCallback` function
- We then use jQuery within `page.evaluate` (via `getText`) to retrieve values from the page

The remaining contents of the file (`verify` and `handleError`) ensure that PhantomJS writes all errors to the console and sets an appropriate exit code in the case of a failure.

# Summary

In this chapter, we have learned how to write unit tests in Node.js, used Mocha and Chai to write more descriptive tests, created test doubles using Sinon.JS, written application level tests using SuperAgent and SuperTest, and implemented a full-stack test in PhantomJS.

Although we have tests at each layer of our application now, we haven't yet covered all of our code. It would be useful to find any gaps where we should write more tests. We also have to invoke a few different commands to run all of our unit and integration tests. In the next chapter, we'll see how to automate these and other processes as part of a continuous integration build.

# 7
# Setting up an Automated Build

In the previous chapter, we took a major step from a demo application to a maintainable codebase by starting to write automated tests. Another important component of real-world software projects is build automation.

Automated builds allow a whole team to work on a project in a consistent manner. A standardized way of executing common tasks makes it easier for new developers to get started. It also avoids annoying issues with developers getting different results for spurious reasons.

In this chapter, we will cover the following topics:

- Configuring an integration server to build and run our tests automatically
- Setting up an automated task runner to simplify the execution of our tests
- Automating more tasks to help maintain coding standards and test coverage

## Setting up an integration server

Build and test automation allow code changes to be verified by an **integration server**, an automated server independent of individual developers' machines. This helps keep the project stable by catching errors or regressions early on. The integration server can automatically alert the developer who introduced the problem. They then have a chance to fix the problem before it causes issues for the rest of the team or the project as a whole.

Building the codebase and running tests automatically on each commit is called **Continuous Integration** (CI). There are many CI/build servers available. These can be self-hosted or provided as a third-party service. Examples that you may have used before include Jenkins (formerly Hudson), Atlassian Bamboo, JetBrains TeamCity, and Microsoft's Team Foundation Server.

We're going to be using Travis CI (`https://travis-ci.org/`), which is a hosted service for running automated builds. It is free for use with public source code repositories. In order to use Travis CI's free service, we need to host our application's code in a public GitHub repository.

# Setting up a public GitHub repository

If you have your own version of the example application code from following along with the book so far, and are already familiar with GitHub, you can push your code to a new GitHub repository of your own. Otherwise, you can fork one of the example chapter repositories.

Use `https://github.com/NodeJsForDevelopers/chapter06/` if you want to follow along with the changes in this chapter. This contains the example code from the end of *Chapter 6, Testing Node.js Applications*, which we will build on in this chapter. You can create your own fork of this repository using the **Fork** button on GitHub. This should be visible at the top-right of the screen when visiting the URL mentioned earlier:

This will create a new repository under your own GitHub account, using the example code as a starting point.

This is all you need to get started in this chapter. However, if you are not already familiar with Git and/or GitHub and would like to know more, you can find more information at `https://help.github.com/`.

# Building a project on Travis CI

We'll now set up a build for our application on Travis CI. If you created your own public repository in the previous section, you can try this out for yourself. Visit `https://travis-ci.org` and sign in with GitHub. You should see a profile page listing your repositories. Enable the repository you just created.

We have to create a simple `config` file to tell Travis CI in what environment(s) to build our application. Create a file in the root of the project as follows (note the leading dot in the file name `.travis.yml`):

```
language: node_js
node_js:
  - 6
  - 4
```

This tells TravisCI to build our project with the current stable and long-term support versions of Node.js (at the time of writing). If you're familiar with Git, you can make this change in a local clone of your repository, commit, and push it to master. If you're new to Git, the easiest way to create this file is to navigate to your repository on `https://github.com` and click on the **New file** button. This will open a web-based editor from which you can create and commit the file.

Once you have added this file to your repository, visit `https://travis-ci.org` again. You should now see a passing build for your repository:

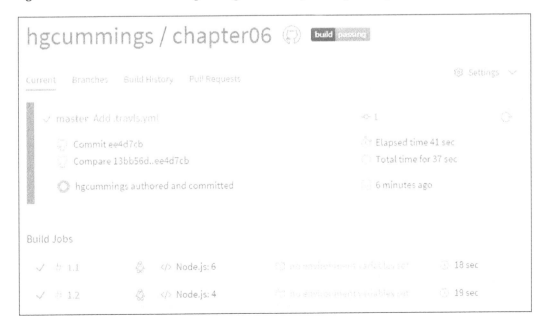

TravisCI built our project twice, once for each version of Node.js that we specified. If you click on either build you can see the command-line output. Notice that TravisCI automatically ran our tests using the standard `npm test` command.

# Automating the build process with Gulp

It's great that TravisCI runs our tests automatically. But that's not the only task we want to automate. Of course, as JavaScript is an interpreted language, we don't have a compile step in our build process. There are other tasks we want to carry out though, for example, checking our code style, running integration tests, and gathering code coverage. We can make use of a build tool to automate these tasks and allow us to run them in a consistent manner. You may have used MSBuild for this in .NET before or Java tools such as Maven or Gradle.

There are several different build tools available for Node.js. The two most popular by far are Grunt and Gulp. Both have large communities and an extensive range of plugins for performing different operations. Grunt's model has each operation reading in files and writing back to the filesystem. Gulp uses Node.js streams to pipe processing from one operation to the next.

Grunt's model is slightly simpler and may be easier to get started with, especially if you have modest build requirements. Gulp's model is potentially faster for some types of task and can reduce the amount of build configuration code you need to write. Both are excellent, well-supported build tools. We'll be using Gulp, but everything we do in this chapter could be achieved with Grunt as well.

## Running tests using Gulp

We first need to install Gulp, both globally (to add it to our path) and into the project. Then we add Gulp plugins for controlling Mocha and environment variables:

```
> npm install -g gulp-cli
> npm install gulp@~3.x --save-dev
> npm install gulp-mocha --save-dev
> npm install gulp-env --save-dev
```

We now add a configuration file for Gulp to our project. Gulp will look for a file with this name by convention as `gulpfile.js`:

```
'use strict';

const gulp = require('gulp');
const mocha = require('gulp-mocha');
```

```
const env = require('gulp-env');

gulp.task('test', function() {
  env({ vars: { NODE_ENV: 'test' } });
  return gulp.src('test/**/*.js')
    .pipe(mocha());
});

gulp.task('default', ['test']);
```

This creates a test task and makes an empty default task to run it. The `'default'` task name is special and will be invoked when we run `gulp` from the command line. We can now remove our test script from `package.json` and update our `.travis.yml` file to run Gulp:

```
language: node_js
before_script:
  - npm install -g gulp
script: gulp
node_js:
  - 6
  - 4
```

This hasn't gained us much yet. We now just have a slightly shorter command to execute our tests. However, the use of a build tool will become more valuable as we add more tasks to automate. Let's look at some of the other processes we may want to make part of our build.

# Checking code style with ESLint

Although we don't need a compiler, we can still benefit from having the computer perform static analysis of our code. Linting tools are common in many languages for spotting common programming errors that may lead to subtle bugs or confusing code. You may be familiar with CodeRush, StyleCop, and others for .NET, or CheckStyle, Findbugs, Sonar, and others for Java.

We'll be using a JavaScript/ECMAScript linting tool called ESLint. Let's first install it globally:

```
> npm install -g eslint
```

Now create a config file to tell ESLint what rules to use as `.eslintrc.json`:

```
{
    "extends": "eslint:recommended",
    "env": {
        "node": true,
        "es6": true,
        "mocha": true,
        "browser": true,
        "jquery": true
    },
    "rules": {
        "semi": [2, "always"],
        "quotes": [2, "single"]
    }
}
```

Here, we tell ESLint to use its standard recommended rules for the environments that we are using in our scripts. We also tell it to check for semicolons at the ends of statements and to prefer single quotes. You can run ESLint as follows:

```
> eslint **/*.js
```

ESLint outputs any errors it finds, including the following:

- An unused `favicon` local variable in app.js
- The unused `next` parameter in various middleware functions
- The use of `console.log` in our PhantomJS integration test
- The use of the `phantom` variable in our PhantomJS integration test

The first of these is trivial to solve: we can just remove the variable declaration (this was created for us by the express application template in *Chapter 2, Getting Started with Node.js*). We could do the same for the `next` parameters on our middleware functions. However, I prefer middleware functions to have a standard and easily identifiable signature. Instead of removing this parameter, we can tell ESLint to ignore this particular parameter as follows:

```
    "rules": {
        "semi": [2, "always"],
        "quotes": [2, "single"],
        "no-unused-vars": [2, {"argsIgnorePattern": "next"}]
    }
```

The last two bullet points both relate to our PhantomJS integration test. This is quite a special file, so here we'll change ESLint's behavior for this file specifically, using a comment directive. We can add the following directives at the very top of the offending file, `integration-test/game.js`:

```
/*eslint-env phantomjs */
/*eslint-disable no-console */
```

The first of these directives tells ESLint that this script file will run in the PhantomJS environment, where the `phantom` variable will be provided for us, so ESLint does not need to warn us against referencing it. The second directive disable's ESLint's rule against using console logging.

If you run ESLint again, you should find that the errors listed previously have disappeared. Any remaining errors should be smaller issues such as missing semicolons or inconsistent use of quotes. These should be quick to fix manually, but in fact, ESLint can do this for us, as we'll see in the next section.

# Automatically fixing issues in ESLint

ESLint is able to automatically correct some of the issues it finds. If ESLint is not currently reporting any errors, try removing a semicolon from one of the project's source files. Run ESLint and you should see an error for this.

Now run ESLint with the `--fix` option as follows:

```
> eslint **/*.js --fix
```

ESLint replaces the semicolon for us. Not all of ESLint's rules can be fixed in this way, but many of them can. It depends on whether a rule's errors always have a single unambiguous fix. The full list of rules, including which ones are fixable, can be found on the ESLint site at `http://eslint.org/docs/rules/`.

You should now be able to run ESLint with no errors or warnings. ESLint is now ready to pick up errors in any new code that we write.

# Running ESLint from Gulp

It's slightly messy to specify special exclusions for our Phantom integration test. It's also unfortunate that we're enabling the Node.js, Mocha, browser, and jQuery environments globally. The Mocha environment is only needed for our test code. The browser and jQuery environments are only need for our client-side code, where the Node.js environment is not needed.

This would be easier to manage if we ran ESLint separately on different sets of files. This would start to become tedious and error-prone if we did it manually. But it's a great use case for a build tool. We can set up separate ESLint profiles for different sets of files using Gulp. First, install the Gulp ESLint plugin:

```
> npm install gulp-eslint --save-dev
```

Now we can create Gulp tasks to lint each set of sources. By default, the `gulp-eslint` plugin uses rules from our `.eslintrc.json` file. So, we can cut this down to just the rules that are relevant to all sources:

```json
{
    "extends": "eslint:recommended",
    "rules": {
        "no-unused-vars": [2, { "args": "after-used" }],
        "quotes": [2, "single"],
        "semi": [2, "always"]
    }
}
```

We can then specify the relevant rules or environments for each set of sources in their own Gulp task. This also allows us to remove the special directive comments from the top of our integration test script:

```javascript
const eslint = require('gulp-eslint');

gulp.task('lint-server', function() {
    return gulp.src(['src/**/*.js', '!src/public/**/*.js'])
        .pipe(eslint({
            envs: [ 'es6', 'node' ],
            rules: {
                'no-unused-vars': [2, {'argsIgnorePattern': 'next'}]
            }
        }))
        .pipe(eslint.format())
        .pipe(eslint.failAfterError());
});

gulp.task('lint-client', function() {
    return gulp.src('src/public/**/*.js')
        .pipe(eslint({ envs: [ 'browser', 'jquery' ] }))
        .pipe(eslint.format())
        .pipe(eslint.failAfterError());
});
```

```
gulp.task('lint-test', function() {
    return gulp.src('test/**/*.js')
        .pipe(eslint({ envs: [ 'es6', 'node', 'mocha' ] }))
        .pipe(eslint.format())
        .pipe(eslint.failAfterError());
});

gulp.task('lint-integration-test', function() {
    return gulp.src('integration-test/**/*.js')
        .pipe(eslint({
            envs: [ 'browser', 'phantomjs', 'jquery' ],
            rules: { 'no-console': 0 }
        }))
        .pipe(eslint.format())
        .pipe(eslint.failAfterError());
});
```

Finally, we wire up the dependencies between our tasks:

```
gulp.task('test', ['lint-test'], function() {
  env({ vars: { NODE_ENV: 'test' } });
  return gulp.src('test/**/*.js')
    .pipe(mocha());
});

gulp.task('lint', [
  'lint-server', 'lint-client', 'lint-test', 'lint-integration-test'
]);
gulp.task('default', ['lint', 'test']);
```

Here, we make the test task depend on lint-test and create a new overall lint task to run all of the others as part of the default build. Try running Gulp and observe the output. Note that it kicks off all the lint tasks in parallel, but waits for lint-test to complete before running tests. By default, Gulp will run tasks concurrently if possible. If a task returns a stream (the object obtained from gulp.src) at the end, Gulp is able to use this to detect when the task finishes. Gulp will wait for a task to finish before starting any tasks that depend on it.

To see how ESLint failures affect Gulp, let's add another ESLint rule to ensure the use of JavaScript's strict mode, as described in *Chapter 3, A JavaScript Primer*. The following code is from `.eslintrc.json`:

```
{
    "extends": "eslint:recommended",
    "rules": {
        "no-unused-vars": [2, { "args": "after-used" }],
        "quotes": [2, "single"],
        "semi": [2, "always"],
        "strict": [2, "safe"]
    }
}
```

ESLint is clever enough to make use of the specified environment for each set of files to work out how strict mode should be applied: at the top of functions for client-side scripts and globally for files that will become Node.js modules. It also spots when we unnecessarily specify strict mode multiple times, globally or in nested functions.

When you execute Gulp, notice that failures in the ESLint tasks prevent the dependent test tasks from running. If you fix the strict mode errors, then Gulp will run successfully again.

# Gathering code coverage statistics

Although we have some tests for our application, they are certainly not yet comprehensive. It would be useful to be able to see what parts of our code are covered by tests. For this, we'll use Istanbul, a JavaScript code coverage tool. First, install the `gulp-instanbul` plugin:

```
> npm install gulp-istanbul --save-dev
```

Now we need to add a Gulp task to instrument our production code for coverage:

```
const istanbul = require('gulp-istanbul');

...

gulp.task('instrument', function() {
    return gulp.src('src/**/*.js')
        .pipe(istanbul())
        .pipe(istanbul.hookRequire())
});
```

Finally, we need to update our test task to output a coverage report and fail the build if we are below our threshold:

```
gulp.task('test', ['lint-test', 'instrument'], function() {
    gulp.src('test/**/*.js')
        .pipe(mocha())
        .pipe(istanbul.writeReports())
        .pipe(istanbul.enforceThresholds({
            thresholds: { global:90 }
        }));
});
```

Now, when we run Gulp, three new results occur:

- A coverage summary appears on the command line
- A set of coverage reports appear under the coverage folder
- The build fails because we are below the coverage threshold

The build summary on the command line is very useful. There is even more detail in the HTML report that appears at coverage/lcov-report/index.html (in the project directory).

Although we need to improve our test coverage, we don't want to leave our build failing. For now, we'll set the coverage target just below our current level so it doesn't drop further. We can do this with the options passed to istanbul.enforceThresholds:

```
gulp.task('test', ['lint-test', 'instrument'], function() {
    return gulp.src('test/**/*.js')
        .pipe(mocha())
        .pipe(istanbul.writeReports())
        .pipe(istanbul.enforceThresholds({
            thresholds: {
                global: {
                    statements: 70,
                    branches: 50
                }
            }
        }));
});
```

# Running integration tests from Gulp

Gulp tasks are just ordinary JavaScript functions, so can contain any functionality we like. Let's look at a more complex use case. We'll create a task that starts up our server, runs integration tests, and then closes the server. For this, we'll need the Gulp Shell plugin:

```
> npm install gulp-shell --save-dev
```

First, we update our integration test script so that we can pass in the port number of the test server. This makes use of the PhantomJS 'system' module as follows (in integration-test/game.js):

```
var rootUrl = 'http://localhost:' +
                require('system').env.TEST_PORT || 3000;
```

Now we can define a Gulp task to run the server and the integration test:

```
const shell = require('gulp-shell');

...

gulp.task('integration-test',
          ['lint-integration-test', 'test'], (done) => {
  const TEST_PORT = 5000;
  let server = require('http')
    .createServer(require('./src/app.js'))
    .listen(TEST_PORT, function() {
      gulp.src('integration-test/**/*.js')
        .pipe(shell('node node_modules/phantomjs-prebuilt/bin/
phantomjs <%=file.path%>', {
            env: { 'TEST_PORT': TEST_PORT }
        }))
        .on('error', () => server.close(done))
        .on('end', () => server.close(done))
    });
});
```

This launches the application and then makes use of the gulp-shell plugin to execute our integration test scripts. Finally, we make sure we close the server when done, passing in Gulp's async callback. Like returning a stream, using this callback allows Gulp to know when the task has completed.

We make this task depend on the `test` task so that they don't interfere with one another. We don't make this part of our default task as it's a more heavyweight operation. We do want it to run on our build server though, so we'll add it to `.travis.yml` along with the default task:

```
language: node_js
before_script:
  - npm install -g gulp
script: gulp default integration-test
node_js:
  - 5
  - 4
```

Now, if we push to the remote master, TravisCI will run static analysis on our code, execute all of our unit and integration tests, and check the unit test coverage.

# Summary

In this chapter, we have set up an integration build using Travis CI, added static analysis of our code using ESLint, automated our tests and other tasks using Gulp, and started measuring our test coverage using the Istanbul tool.

Now that we have the infrastructure in place for stable development, we can start expanding our project. In the next chapter, we'll introduce persistent data stores to the application.

# 8
# Mastering Asynchronicity

Our JavaScript primer (*Chapter 3, A JavaScript Primer*) covered all the important concepts to let us start building our application. But there is one fundamental aspect of JavaScript programming worth exploring in more detail: asynchronicity.

*Chapter 1, Why Node.js?*, discussed the asynchronous programming model of Node.js. It described the consistent approach used throughout Node.js APIs and third-party libraries. Recall that each asynchronous method takes a callback function that gets passed error and result arguments, for example, the `fs.stat` function we saw in *Chapter 1, Why Node.js?*:

```
fs.stat('/hello/world', function (error, stats) {
  console.log('File last updated at: ' + stats.mtime);
});
```

However, the callback pattern has some weaknesses. Performing error handling and combining results from multiple asynchronous operations can become quite clumsy. There are alternative asynchronous patterns available in JavaScript that address these issues. The idea of multiple competing patterns might seem worrying in itself, though. Having a single consistent approach was one of the benefits of Node.js discussed in *Chapter 1, Why Node.js?*.

We should also revisit the idea of Node.js APIs and libraries being asynchronous throughout. We need to consider how this applies to our own code. This is not just something we need to worry about if writing a module for use by a third-party. Even within our own applications, most modules will need to expose their functionality through an asynchronous interface. If not, we severely limit the freedom of how we implement these modules.

In this chapter, we will cover the following topics:

- Introducing asynchronous interfaces to our own modules
- Observing some of the weaknesses of the callback pattern
- Refactoring away from callbacks to make our asynchronous code more readable
- Seeing how we can still benefit from the consistency of Node.js's asynchronous programming model

# Using the callback pattern for asynchronous code

Let's look at one of the methods from our games service:

```
module.exports.get = (id) => games.find(game => game.id === id);
```

The interface of this function is synchronous: you call it and get a value back. *Chapter 4*, *Introducing Node.js Modules*, introduced the games service as the module responsible for how we store our games. The interface shouldn't need to change if we change the storage implementation. This isn't quite the case at the moment, though.

As discussed before, most Node.js libraries are asynchronous. Synchronous interfaces can't make use of asynchronous implementations. Let's say the `get` function wants to make use of an asynchronous method in a third-party `datastore` library. What would that look like? The comments in the following (non-working) code describe the problem:

```
module.exports.get = (id) => {
    datastore.getById(id, (err, result) => {
        // Result available, but outer method has already returned
    });
    return ???; // Need to return here, but have no result yet
};
```

This is a problem in general, not just in JavaScript. In other platforms, you could delay returning until the asynchronous operation has completed. This turns an asynchronous operation into a blocking operation. In Node.js (and other JavaScript environments), blocking in this way is not an option. It would be incompatible with the single-threaded, non-blocking, event-driven execution model.

# Exposing the callback pattern

To allow our games service to be able to make use of asynchronous libraries, we need to give it an asynchronous interface. Note that almost all libraries in the Node.js ecosystem are asynchronous. If they weren't, they would be limited in the same way as our games service currently is.

We can rewrite the interface of our `get` function to follow the standard asynchronous callback pattern. Let's see what effect this has on using an asynchronous third-party `datastore` library (again, this is non-working code, with a fictional `datastore` object):

```
module.exports.get = (id, callback) => {
  datastore.getById(id, (err, result) => {
    // Can now make use of the result by passing to the callback
    callback(err, result);
  }
  // No longer need to return here
}
```

Of course, in this case we could simplify the preceding code as follows:

```
module.exports.get = (id, callback) => {
    datastore.getById(id, callback);
}
```

In general, though, we might want to do some more processing of the result from a third-party library. So our function might look more like this:

```
module.exports.get = (id, callback) => {
    datastore.getById(id, (err, result) => {
        if (err) {
            callback(err);
        } else {
            callback(null, processResult(result));
        }
    }
}
```

Assuming `processResult` is internal to our module, it's fine for it to have a synchronous interface for now. If it needs to do asynchronous work later, we can change its interface without affecting the consumers of our module.

Our games service module's *public* interface does need to be entirely asynchronous, though. We're not actually changing the implementation of the module yet. This makes updating the interface quite straightforward. We can make the following changes in `src/services/games.js`:

```
'use strict';

const games = [];
let nextId = 1;

class Game {
    ...

    remove(callback) {
        games.splice(games.indexOf(this), 1);
        callback();
    }
}

module.exports.create = (userId, word, callback) => {
    const newGame = new Game(nextId++, userId, word);
    games.push(newGame);
    callback(newGame);
};
module.exports.get = (id, callback) =>
    callback(null,
        games.find(game => game.id === parseInt(id, 10)));
module.exports.createdBy = (userId, callback) =>
    callback(null, games.filter(game => game.setBy === userId));
module.exports.availableTo = (userId, callback) =>
    callback(null, games.filter(game => game.setBy !== userId));
```

Note that this is slightly unrealistic, though. Control would normally return to the caller before an asynchronous method completes. We can achieve this by using `process.nextTick` to schedule the execution of the callback on the next tick of the event loop (refer to *Chapter 1, Why Node.js?*, if you want a refresher on the event loop):

```
'use strict';

const games = [];
let nextId = 1;

const asAsync = (callback, result) =>
            process.nextTick(() => callback(null, result));
```

```
class Game {
    ...

    remove(callback) {
        games.splice(games.indexOf(this), 1);
        asAsync(callback);
    }
}

module.exports.create = (userId, word, callback) => {
    let game = new Game(nextId++, userId, word);
    games.push(game);
    asAsync(callback);
};
module.exports.get = (id, callback) =>
    asAsync(callback,
        games.find(game => game.id === parseInt(id, 10)));
module.exports.createdBy = (userId, callback) =>
    asAsync(callback, games.filter(game => game.setBy === userId));
module.exports.availableTo = (userId, callback) =>
    asAsync(callback, games.filter(game => game.setBy !== userId));
```

Updating the rest of our application to consume this asynchronous interface is a trickier task. This is why it is worth always writing module interfaces to be asynchronous from the start. We should definitely address this before expanding our application any further.

# Consuming asynchronous interfaces

The games service is called by the games route, the index route, and by our tests. Let's look at the corresponding changes to each of these in turn. The following code is from `src/routes/games.js`:

```
'use strict';

const express = require('express');
const router = express.Router();
const service = require('../service/games.js');

router.post('/', function(req, res, next) {
    let word = req.body.word;
    if (word && /^[A-Za-z]{3,}$/.test(word)) {
        service.create(req.user.id, word, (err, game) => {
            if (err) {
```

```
                next(err);
            } else {
                res.redirect(`/games/${game.id}/created`);
            }
        });
    } else {
        res.status(400).send('Word must be at least three characters
long and contain only letters');
    }
});

const checkGameExists = function(id, res, onSuccess, onError) {
    service.get(id, function(err, game) {
        if (err) {
            onError(err);
        } else {
            if (game) {
                onSuccess(game);
            } else {
                res.status(404).send('Non-existent game ID');
            }
        }
    });
};

router.get('/:id', function(req, res, next) {
    checkGameExists(
        req.params.id,
        res,
        game => { ... },
        next);
});

router.post('/:id/guesses', function(req, res, next) {
    checkGameExists(
        req.params.id,
        res,
        game => { ... },
        next);
});

router.delete('/:id', function(req, res, next) {
    checkGameExists(
        req.params.id,
```

```
            res,
            game => {
                if (game.setBy === req.user.id) {
                    game.remove((err) => {
                        if (err) {
                            next(err);
                        } else {
                            res.send();
                        }
                    });
                } else {
                    res.status(403).send('You don't have permission...');
                }
            },
            next);
    });

    router.get('/:id/created', function(req, res, next) {
        checkGameExists(
            req.params.id,
            res,
            game => res.render('createdGame', game),
            next);
    });

    module.exports = router;
```

In this case, the changes are straightforward. Each call to a games service function now passes in a callback. The callback contains the logic that used to follow the call to the games service function. Each callback also needs to handle the possibility of an error value. In this case, we simply pass it to the Express `next` callback so it will be handled by our global error handler.

Although these changes are straightforward, they have introduced some repetitive boilerplate to our code. This is even more of a problem in the index route; take a look at the code from `src/routes/index.js`:

```
var express = require('express');
var router = express.Router();
var games = require('../service/games.js');

router.get('/', function(req, res, next) {
  games.createdBy(req.user.id, (err, createdGames) => {
    if (err) {
      next(err);
```

```
      } else {
        games.availableTo(req.user.id, (err, availableGames) => {
          if (err) {
            next(err);
          } else {
            res.render('index', {
              title: 'Hangman',
              userId: req.user.id,
              createdGames: createdGames,
              availableGames: availableGames,
              partials: { createdGame: 'createdGame' }
            });
          }
        });
      }
    });});

  module.exports = router;
```

Here, we need to combine the result of two different asynchronous calls. This leads to nested callbacks. We also have to repeat the error-handling code at each stage. Note also that we only start the second asynchronous operation after the first one completes. It would be better to start the operations in parallel.

Recall that, while JavaScript itself is single-threaded, asynchronous operations may perform work in parallel, for example, network, disk, and other I/O operations. Running multiple operations in parallel would need even more complicated (and error-prone) boilerplate code. For an example of how this might work, consider the changes to make the beforeEach function in the games service test asynchronous. The following code is from src/test/services/games.js:

```
describe('Game service', function() {
    let firstUserId = 'user-id-1';
    let secondUserId = 'user-id-2';

    beforeEach(function(done) {
        service.availableTo('not-a-user', (err, gamesAdded) => {
            let gamesDeleted = 0;
            if (gamesAdded.length === 0) {
                done();
            }
            gamesAdded.forEach(game => {
                game.remove(() => {
                    if (++gamesDeleted === gamesAdded.length) {
                        done();
```

```
                    }
                });
            });
        });
    });


    . . .

});
```

Here, we need to make an unknown number of calls to the asynchronous remove method. The `done` callback must be invoked when they are all complete. There are several ways of achieving this, but they all involve additional boilerplate. The approach here is the simplest possible, keeping count of the number of complete operations. Also note that we are omitting error handling, since this is test code. In production code, we would have to worry about error handling as well, making things even more complicated.

>  There are other changes to the tests to make use of the new asynchronous interface of the games service. They are excluded here for brevity. They are similar to the changes in `index.js`. You can see a full set of changes by viewing this chapter's first commit in the Git repository at `https://github.com/NodeJsForDevelopers/chapter08`.

This all seems quite unsatisfactory. Our code has become more complicated, repetitive, and harder to read. Fortunately, we can address these issues by using a different approach to writing asynchronous code.

# Writing cleaner asynchronous code using promises

**Promises** are an alternative pattern to callbacks for writing asynchronous code. A promise represents an operation that hasn't completed yet but is expected to do so in the future. As the name *promise* suggests, a promise is a contract to eventually provide a value or a reason for failure (that is, an error). You may already be familiar with this pattern from Tasks in .NET or Futures in Java. A promise has three possible states:

- **pending** represents an in-progress operation
- **fulfilled** representing a successful operation, with a result value
- **rejected** representing an unsuccessful operation, with a failure reason

When executing a single operation, the callback-based and promise-based approaches appear quite similar. The power of promises comes when combining asynchronous operations.

Consider an example where we have asynchronous library functions for obtaining, processing, and aggregating data. We want to perform these operations in turn then display the result, handling errors as we go. Using callbacks, it might look like this (in non-runnable, fictional code):

```
lib.getInitialData(function(e, initialData) {
  if (e) {
    console.log('Error: ' + e);
  } else {
    lib.processData(initialData, (e, processedData) => {
      if (e) {
        console.log('Error: ' + e);
      } else {
        lib.aggregateData(processedData, (e, aggregatedData) => {
          if (e) {
            console.log('Error: ' + e);
          } else {
            console.log('Success! Result=' + aggregatedData);
          }
        });
      }
    });
  }
});
```

This has many of the same problems we encountered in our own code in the previous section: nested callbacks, extra boilerplate, and repetitive error-handling. If these functions instead returned promises, the equivalent of the above code would be as follows:

```
lib.getInitialData()
    .then(lib.processData)
    .then(lib.aggregateData)
    .then(function(aggregatedData) {
        console.log('Success! Result=' + result);
    }, function(error) {
        console.log('Error: ' + error);
    });
```

The then function applies a function to the resulting value of a promise, returning a new promise. In this way, we construct a chain of promises representing a series of operations.

The then function takes two arguments, which are both callbacks. If the asynchronous operation returns an error, the second argument will be invoked instead. In the above example, if the `library.aggregateData` call fails, then we will log an error.

If the second then callback parameter is omitted, any errors propagate along the chain of promises. In the above example, this means that if the `library.processData` call fails, then `library.aggregateData` will not be called and our error-logging callback will still be invoked.

If you only care about the error case, you can just specify an error callback using the catch function instead of then. You can also use this together with propagation to rewrite the preceding code more clearly:

```
library.getInitialData()
    .then(library.processData)
    .then(library.aggregateData)
    .then(function(aggregatedData) {
        console.log('Success! Result=' + result);
    })
    .catch(function(error) {
        console.log('Error: ' + error);
    });
```

Here, errors at any point propagate to a final promise which we check for errors. Note that this rewritten version would also catch any errors thrown by our success-logging callback, which the preceding version would not have done. You should always call catch at the end of a promise chain, unless you are returning the resulting promise object to be consumed elsewhere.

# Implementing promise-based asynchronous code

Let's apply the promise pattern to our existing application. First, we'll need to update our game service API to expose promises instead of callbacks. As before, this is straightforward since our game service doesn't actually use any asynchronous operations in its implementation (yet). A promised-based version of our games service looks like the following (in `src/services/games.js`):

```
'use strict';

const games = [];
let currentId = 1;

class Game {
```

```
        ...

    remove() {
        games.splice(games.indexOf(this), 1);
        return Promise.resolve();
    }
}

module.exports.create = (userId, word) => {
    const newGame = new Game(nextId++, userId, word);
    games.push(newGame);
    return Promise.resolve(newGame);
};
module.exports.get = (id) =>
    Promise.resolve(
        games.find(game => game.id === parseInt(id, 10)));
module.exports.createdBy = (userId) =>
    Promise.resolve(games.filter(game => game.setBy === userId));
module.exports.availableTo = (userId) =>
    Promise.resolve(games.filter(game => game.setBy !== userId));
```

Creating a promise-based interface is even simpler than a callback-based one. We can create a promise for an already known value using the `Promise.resolve()` function. Each function in our games service looks much like the original synchronous version, just with an extra call to `Promise.resolve`.

If you pass a promise argument to `Promise.resolve`, then you get back a promise that behaves like the original argument. If you pass any other value, you get an already resolved promise for that value. This can be useful if you need to operate on a variable that might be a promise or a value. You can pass it to `Promise.resolve`, then treat it consistently as a promise.

## Consuming the promise pattern

Now we need to update the rest of our codebase to use promises. Let's look through the same files as before, starting with the games route. See the following code from `src/routes/games.js`:

```
'use strict';

const express = require('express');
const router = express.Router();
const service = require('../service/games.js');
```

```
router.post('/', function(req, res, next) {
    let word = req.body.word;
    if (word && /^[A-Za-z]{3,}$/.test(word)) {
        service.create(req.user.id, word)
            .then(game =>
                res.redirect(`/games/${game.id}/created`))
            .catch(next);
    } else {
        res.status(400).send('Word must be at least three characters
long and contain only letters');
    }
});

const checkGameExists = function(id, res, onSuccess, onError) {
    service.get(id)
        .then(game => {
            if (game) {
                onSuccess(game);
            } else {
                res.status(404).send('Non-existent game ID');
            }
        })
        .catch(onError);
};

...

router.delete('/:id', function(req, res, next) {
    checkGameExists(
        req.params.id,
        res,
        game => {
            if (game.setBy === req.user.id) {
                game.remove()
                    .then(() => res.send())
                    .catch(next);
            } else {
                res.status(403).send('You do not have permission to
delete this game');
            }
        },
        next);
});
```

This file was the simplest before, so shows the least difference here. We still have a little repetition of boilerplate (for example, the `catch` call). Still, the promise-based approach is more compact and readable than with callbacks. Now let's look at the index route code from `src/routes/index.js`:

```
var express = require('express');
var router = express.Router();
var games = require('../service/games.js');

router.get('/', function(req, res, next) {
    games.createdBy(req.user.id)
        .then(gamesCreatedByUser =>
            games.availableTo(req.user.id)
                .then(gamesAvailableToUser => {
                    res.render('index', {
                        title: 'Hangman',
                        userId: req.user.id,
                        createdGames: gamesCreatedByUser,
                        availableGames: gamesAvailableToUser
                    });
                }))
        .catch(next);
});

module.exports = router;
```

This is a little better. There is less repetition, but still some nesting and boilerplate. Note that the outermost `then` callback returns a promise (chained from `games.availableTo`). When a `then` callback returns a promise, this is effectively flattened, so the overall promise returns the value of the inner promise. This flattening also applies to the propagation of errors, so we don't need to call `catch` on the inner promise explicitly.

This code is still a little confusing to follow. There is actually a way to make it much more readable, which we'll come back to shortly. Let's first look at the `beforeEach` function in the games service test in the following code from `test/service/games.js`:

```
describe('Game service', function() {
    let firstUserId = 'user-id-1';
    let secondUserId = 'user-id-2';

    beforeEach(function(done) {
        service.availableTo('non-existent-user')
            .then(games => games.map(game => game.remove()))
            .then(gamesRemoved => Promise.all(gamesRemoved))
```

```
                .then(() => done(), done);
        });
    });
```

This has become much shorter and more linear. Let's break down what each line does:

- `service.availableTo` returns a promise of an array of games
- The first `then` callback uses `array.map` to convert this into a *promise of an array of promises* of delete operations
- The next `then` callback uses `Promise.all` to convert this into a single promise for the whole array of delete operations

> The `Promise.all` function takes an array of promises and returns a promise that resolves when all of the promises in the array have resolved or is rejected as soon as any promise in the array is rejected.

- The final `then` callback is invoked when the promise returned from `Promise.all` resolves, that is, when all the delete operations are complete, and invokes Mocha's `done` callback

Note that unlike with the callback-based approach, it is also trivial to implement error handling. We just pass in the `done` callback as the error handler (second argument) to the final `then` call. We can take a similar approach in the tests themselves as we've done here with the `beforeEach` callback. Again, the updates to the tests are omitted for brevity, but you can find them in the book's companion code.

# Parallelising operations using promises

We can also make use of the `Promise.all` function to simplify the index route. Recall that our code is invoking the two asynchronous operations one after the other. In the callback-based approach, attempting to execute these in parallel would have made the code even more complicated. With promises, it actually makes our code more readable:

```
var express = require('express');
var router = express.Router();
var games = require('../service/games.js');

router.get('/', function(req, res, next) {
    Promise.all([
        games.createdBy(req.user.id),
```

```
            games.availableTo(req.user.id)
    ])
        .then(results => {
            res.render('index', {
                        title: 'Hangman',
                        userId: req.user.id,
                        createdGames: results[0],
                        availableGames: results[1]
                    });
                })
        .catch(next);
});

module.exports = router;
```

This is shorter and much easier to understand. We kick off two asynchronous operations to load data, then make use of the data as soon as both operations have completed.

> The only slight drawback of the preceding approach is that we have to get each of the two values back out of the array by their index. In Node.js v6 or higher, we could avoid this and make the code more readable still by using **destructuring** to assign two named parameters from the values in the array, as follows:
> ```
> .then(([created, available]) => { ...
> ```
> This isn't used in the example above for back-compatibility with Node.js v4. We will discuss destructuring in more detail in *Chapter 14, Node.js and Beyond*.

# Combining asynchronous programming patterns

Promises allow us to address some of the shortcomings of the callback pattern and write more readable code. Now we have a new problem, though. One of the merits of Node.js is the consistent approach to asynchronous programming. We seem to have negated this by introducing promises as well as the conventional callback pattern.

Furthermore, although native promises are new to ECMAScript 2015, the concept is not new. There are many pre-existing libraries that provide their own implementation of promises.

Fortunately, these competing approaches to asynchronous programming are actually very consistent. The biggest value of the consistency in the Node.js-style callback pattern comes from the following:

- All library functions are asynchronous (non-blocking) by default
- All asynchronous operations return a single value or an error

Promises are completely consistent with the above points. There is also excellent compatibility between different implementations of promises in JavaScript. This is thanks to the Promises/A+ specification (`http://promisesaplus.com`). This essentially defines the behavior of the `then` method. Any promise library you are likely to come across will follow this spec. Native JavaScript promises are also designed to be compatible with it. These means that all of these libraries and native JavaScript promises are interoperable.

So all libraries using callbacks follow the same convention and all promise libraries follow the same specification. The only issue remaining is converting between promises and callbacks. There are several promise libraries that can do this for us.

If you just want to convert a few standard callback functions to promises, you can use `denodeify`, which can be installed using npm. Our `fs.stat` example from earlier would look like this:

```
const denodeify = require('denodeify');
const stat = denodeify(require('fs').stat);
stat('/hello/world')
    .then(stats => console.log('File last updated at: ' +
stats.mtime));
```

You will also find that many libraries expose functions that can return a promise or accept a callback and so can be invoked with either pattern.

# Summary

In this chapter, we have seen how to expose the standard Node.js callback interface in our own modules. We have made use of promises to produce more readable asynchronous code. Finally, we have seen how we can use promises together with standard Node.js callbacks.

Now that we can implement our own asynchronous APIs, we can expand on our application and start making use of other libraries that provide asynchronous interfaces. In the next chapter, we will make use of this to introduce persistent storage to our application.

# 9
# Persisting Data

Most applications need to persist some kind of data. In this chapter, we'll be looking at some approaches to data persistence for Node.js applications.

The default choice for persistence for a long time has been the traditional relational database. You may have used **RDBMSs** (relational database management systems) such as Microsoft SQL Server, Oracle, MySQL or PostgreSQL. These systems are often categorized as *SQL databases* since they all use SQL as their primary query language.

More recently, there has been a proliferation of so-called **NoSQL** databases. This umbrella term isn't particularly useful as a category. Some NoSQL databases have no more in common with each other than with traditional relational databases.

What's interesting is the range of databases available and the use cases they fulfil. Traditional RDBMSs are as powerful and flexible as ever and the right choice for many situations. In this chapter, we'll consider two other types of database, along with how and when to make use of them.

The systems we'll be looking at are **MongoDB** and **Redis**. Both of these had their initial release in 2009 and are now widely-used. Covering either of them in depth would justify a book in itself. The aim of this chapter is to provide an introduction to and high-level overview of each.

In this chapter, we will cover the following topics:

- The conceptual data model used by each of these systems
- The use cases for which they provide the most benefit
- Integrating them with an Express application
- Testing data persistence code

# Introducing MongoDB

MongoDB is a **document-oriented** DBMS. MongoDB documents are stored as **binary JSON (BSON)**. This is similar to JSON, but with support for additional data types. JSON field values can only be strings, numbers, objects, arrays, Booleans, or null. BSON supports more specific numeric types, dates and timestamps, regular expressions, and binary data. As the name suggests, BSON documents are stored and transferred as binary data. This can be more efficient than JSON's string representation.

MongoDB documents are stored in **collections**. These work very much like tables in a traditional relational database. Documents can be inserted, updated, and queried. There are two key differences from a traditional relational database:

- MongoDB does not support server-side joins. In a traditional RDBMS, you would normalize data into multiple tables and join across them using foreign keys. In MongoDB, you instead use BSON's nested structure to denormalize data about each entity into a single document.

- The *relational* property of a relational database is that all rows in a table contain the same fields with the same meaning. In MongoDB, documents can have any set of fields.

In practice, documents in the same collection typically have the same fields or at least a common core set of fields. MongoDB supports the creation of indexes on common fields in a collection to make querying more efficient.

# Why choose MongoDB?

There are several properties of MongoDB that make it an appealing choice for some use cases, especially in Node.js-based applications. We'll cover these in this section.

## Object modeling

MongoDB's document-based approach can be a good fit for persisting domain entities. You may have experience of storing domain entities in a relational database using an **Object-Relational Mapper (ORM)**. Hibernate and Entity Framework are popular examples of ORMs. One of the jobs performed by an ORM is mapping a single entity to multiple tables in a normalized schema. When an entity is loaded from the database, it is reconstructed via JOIN queries between these tables. This is one of the key features of ORMs. It is also one of the most common sources of configuration problems and performance issues when using an ORM. MongoDB persists each entity as a single document, which can be much simpler.

Of course, cross-table joins can also be useful for traversing relationships between entities. While ORMs typically make this easy, this can itself be a source of performance problems. Implicit loading of related entities often causes *N+1* problems, issuing thousands of DB queries. Handling these relationships well requires careful thought, whatever kind of database you are using.

When using an ORM and an RDBMS, all inter-entity relationships are foreign keys, but you need to think carefully about how to load them. When modeling data in MongoDB, you must choose between embedded documents or document references for inter-entity relationships. Under either tech stack, the design decisions depend on the data access requirements of your application and designing the data model to reduce the prevalence of inter-entity relationships will simplify matters.

## JavaScript

MongoDB is a good fit for Node.js in particular. The use of a JSON-like format maps well to a JavaScript-based programming environment. MongoDB itself also runs JavaScript natively. Database operations can make use of custom JavaScript functions that execute on the server.

## Scalability

MongoDB also scales in a similar manner to Node.js. It uses partitioning and replication to support horizontal scaling on commodity hardware. There is no technical reason why your application and database have to scale in the same way, but it may be easier to plan for scalability from a business perspective.

When using an RDBMS, it is more straightforward to scale the database vertically. That means provisioning a high-powered database server that can support multiple application servers. This requires more careful planning and more up-front investment than linearly scaling application and database servers horizontally together.

## Getting started with MongoDB

Visit `https://www.mongodb.org/downloads` to download and install the latest version of the MongoDB Community Server edition for your operating system. There are more detailed installation instructions in the user manual at `https://docs.mongodb.org/manual/installation/`.

The commands in the rest of this section make use of executables in MongoDB's /bin directory. You can run the commands in this directory or, better still, add it to your PATH.

Create a directory for MongoDB to store its data. Then start the MongoDB daemon process (that is, service), providing the path of that directory as follows:

```
> mongod --dbpath C:\data\mongodb
```

# Using the MongoDB shell

You can interact with MongoDB from the console using its built-in shell application. You can launch the MongoDB shell by running the mongo command, as follows:

```
> mongo demo
```

This will connect to a database named demo (creating it, if necessary) on the local server. If you don't specify a database, then the shell connects to a database named test.

The first thing to notice is that the shell is just another JavaScript environment. We can try running some of the same commands as at the beginning of *Chapter 2, Getting Started with Node.js*.

```
> function square(x) { return x*x; }
> square(42)
1764
> new Date()
ISODate("2016-01-01T20:05:39.652Z")
> var foo = { bar: "baz" }
> typeof foo
object
> foo.bar
baz
```

Just as Node.js builds on JavaScript in ways that make it more suitable for server-side application development, MongoDB adds features more useful to data persistence. Note that new Date() in the preceding code returns an ISODate, MongoDB's standard datatype for representing dates in BSON documents.

You can quit the console by typing exit at any time.

MongoDB also adds some new global variables for interacting with the database. The most important of these is the db object. Let's try adding some documents to our database. Recall that MongoDB stores documents in collections. To create a new collection, we just need to start inserting documents into it. For a simple example, we'll use the UK bank holidays for 2016. We can populate this collection using the following script:

```
db.holidays.insert(
   { name: "New Year's Day", date: ISODate("2016-01-01") });
db.holidays.insert(
   { name: "Good Friday", date: ISODate("2016-03-25") });
db.holidays.insert(
   { name: "Easter Monday", date: ISODate("2016-03-28") });
db.holidays.insert(
   { name: "Early May bank holiday", date: ISODate("2016-05-02") });
db.holidays.insert(
   { name: "Spring bank holiday", date: ISODate("2016-05-30") });
db.holidays.insert(
   { name: "Summer bank holiday", date: ISODate("2016-08-29") });
db.holidays.insert(
   { name: "Boxing Day", date: ISODate("2016-12-26") });
db.holidays.insert(
   { name: "Christmas Day", date: ISODate("2016-12-27"),
     substitute_for: ISODate("2016-12-25") });
```

Note that Christmas Day falls on a Sunday in 2016, so the bank holiday occurs on the next working day. This gives us a reason to have another field that is only relevant to some documents in the collection.

You could type these insert commands into the console manually, but it's easier to tell MongoDB to load them from a script file:

```
> mongo demo holidays.js --shell
```

The previous command connects to a database named demo, runs the holiday.js script (available in the book's companion code), then opens a shell to allow us to interact with the database. We can view the complete contents of the collection by running the following command in the MongoDB console:

```
> db.holidays.find()
{ "_id" : ObjectId("572f760fffb6888d70c45eeb"), "name" : "New Year's
Day", "date" : ISODate("2016-01-01T00:00:00Z") }

{ "_id" : ObjectId("572f7610ffb6888d70c45eec"), "name" : "Good Friday",
"date" : ISODate("2016-03-25T00:00:00Z") }

...
```

Note that MongoDB has automatically added an `_id` field to each document for us.

 You can see how MongoDB does this by viewing the source of the `insert` method. Just type `db.holidays.insert` into the shell (with no parentheses).

We can pull out records by their `_id` or other single fields:

```
> db.holidays.find({name: "Boxing Day"})
```

This will return any objects that match the object passed to `find`. To look up documents by something other than exact equality, we can use MongoDB's query operators. These are prefixed with the dollar symbol and specified as object properties. For example, to find holidays in the second half of the year, we can use the *greater than or equal to* operator as follows:

```
> db.holidays.find({ date: { $gte: new Date("2016-07-01") }})
```

MongoDB's **aggregation pipeline** allows us to build complex queries from a sequence of operations called **pipeline stages**. It is the closest thing in MongoDB to complex querying in SQL. Here, we count the number of bank holidays in each month using MongoDB's `$group` pipeline stage, which is similar to SQL's GROUP BY clause:

```
> db.holidays.aggregate({
    $group: { _id: { $month: "$date" }, count: { $sum: 1 } }})
```

An odd quirk of the calendar in 2016 means that the Christmas Day Bank Holiday actually comes after Boxing Day (since Christmas Day itself is on a Sunday). In the following example, we order bank holidays by the date of the occasion that they mark (stored in the `$substitute_for` field if different from the date of the bank holiday):

```
> db.holidays.aggregate([
    { $project: { _id: false, name: "$name",
        date: { $ifNull: ["$substitute_for", "$date"] } } },
    { $sort: { date: 1 } }
])
```

The previous pipeline consists of two stages:

- The `$project` stage specifies a set of fields based on the underlying data (similar to SELECT in SQL). Note that the `_id` field is included by default, but we exclude it here.

- The `$sort` stage specifies a sort field and direction (similar to SQL's SORT BY clause). The `1` here indicates an ascending sort order.

We have just scratched the surface here. There are many more pipeline phases available in MongoDB. You can find out more about aggregation in the MongoDB documentation at `https://docs.mongodb.com/manual/core/aggregation-pipeline/`.

MongoDB also has a built-in Map-Reduce function for powerful aggregate data processing using arbitrary JavaScript functions. This is beyond the scope of this book, but you can find out more about Map-Reduce and MongoDB's implementation of it at `https://docs.mongodb.com/manual/core/map-reduce/`.

# Using MongoDB with Express

The games service module in our application currently stores all its data in memory. This worked well enough for demo purposes, but isn't suitable for a real application. We lose all the data whenever the application restarts. It also prevents us from scaling our application across multiple processes. Each instance would have its own game service with different data. Users would see different data depending on which server happened to handle their request.

We're going to update our games service to store its data in MongoDB. For this, we're going to make use of a library called **Mongoose**.

# Persisting objects with Mongoose

Recall that, unlike a relational database, MongoDB does not require documents in the same collection to have the same fields. However, we do typically expect most items within a collection to share at least a common core of fields.

Mongoose is an object modeling library for storing entities in MongoDB. It helps with writing common functionality such as validation, query building, and type casting. It also provides hooks for associating business logic with our entities. These are similar to some of the features provided by ORMs such as Entity Framework or Hibernate. Mongoose itself is not an ORM, though. Recall that object-relational mapping is not relevant for document-oriented databases such as MongoDB.

To use Mongoose, we start by defining a **schema**. This defines the common fields for documents within a MongoDB collection. Returning to our demo application from the preceding chapters, let's install Mongoose and define a schema for our games collection:

```
> npm install mongoose --save
```

The following code is added to `src/services/games.js`:

```
'use strict';

const mongoose = require('mongoose');

const Schema = mongoose.Schema;
const gameSchema = new Schema({
    word: String,
    setBy: String
});
```

The schema defines document fields and specifies the type of each field. To start persisting documents with this schema, we need to create a **model**.

Models are constructors that correspond to a MongoDB collection. Instances of a Mongoose model correspond to documents in that collection. Models also provide functions for modifying the collection. We create a model by specifying the schema and (singular) collection name:

```
const gameSchema = new Schema({
    word: String,
    setBy: String
});

const Game = mongoose.model('Game', gameSchema);
```

The Model constructor replaces our Game class and constructor from before. This class also contained two instance methods: `positionsOf` and `remove`. We can define custom instance methods on a schema, which will be available on all model instances. These must be defined before creating the model:

```
const gameSchema = new Schema({
    word: String,
    setBy: String
});

gameSchema.methods.positionsOf = function(character) {
    let positions = [];
    for (let i in this.word) {
        if (this.word[i] === character.toUpperCase()) {
            positions.push(i);
        }
    }
}
```

```
    return positions;
};
```

```
const Game = mongoose.model('Game', gameSchema);
```

 Note that we use a traditional function definition rather than an arrow function in the preceding code. This is necessary in order for the `this` keyword inside the function to work correctly. See `http://derickbailey.com/2015/09/28/do-es6-arrow-functions-really-solve-this-in-javascript/` for more details.

We don't need to define a `remove` method anymore, because Mongoose provides this automatically. It also provides a `save` method, which we can use for persisting new games:

```
const Game = mongoose.model('Game', gameSchema);

module.exports.create = (userId, word) => {
  let game = new Game({setBy: userId, word: word.toUpperCase()});
  return game.save();
};
```

We don't need to specify an ID anymore, since this is also provided by Mongoose. Note that we do need to specify `word.toUpperCase()`, which used to be in the Game constructor. This isn't a problem, since the constructor is private to our module. No code outside the module can invoke the constructor directly. Where the `toUpperCase` call takes place is just an implementation detail.

Also note that Mongoose's async operations all return promises as an alternative to using callbacks. Mongoose supports both of the asynchronous programming patterns discussed in the previous chapter. Mongoose uses its own implementation of promises. We can configure Mongoose to use ECMAScript 6 promises, though. We also need to tell Mongoose to connect to a MongoDB database. For now, we will hardcode the URL, but we'll see how to make this configurable shortly:

```
const mongoose = require('mongoose');
mongoose.Promise = Promise;
mongoose.connect('mongodb://localhost/hangman');
```

Finally, we need to implement our three methods for retrieving games from the database. We can do this using Mongoose's `find` method:

```
module.exports.create = (userId, word) => {
    . . .
};
```

```
module.exports.createdBy =
    (userId) => Game.find({setBy: userId});
module.exports.availableTo =
    (userId) => Game.find({setBy: { $ne: userId } });
module.exports.get =
    (id) => Game.findById(id);
```

The Mongoose `find` method works like the MongoDB `find` method we saw in the previous section, *Using the MongoDB shell*. It takes a set of MongoDB query conditions and asynchronously provides a list of documents. `findById` takes an ID and asynchronously provides a single document, or null.

Mongoose also provides a `where` method for building up conditions through function calls. The `availableTo` function can be rewritten as follows:

```
module.exports.availableTo =
    (userId) => Game.where('setBy').ne(userId);
```

As long as you still have MongoDB running locally (as described in *Getting started with MongoDB* earlier in the chapter), you should now be able to run the application. Try stopping and restarting the application and notice that games are now persisted between restarts.

# Isolating persistence code

It's useful to integrate with a real database to make sure our persistence code is working. But it's not always appropriate for our tests to be dependent on an external MongoDB instance.

We want developers to be able to check out the code and run the application without needing to run a database instance. Also, external dependencies slow down our tests. MongoDB stores data on disk, so introduces additional I/O work into our tests.

The application should depend on an external database in production. In integration, we want to use a real database on the local server. On development machines, it would be better to use an in-memory database by default. So we need to be able to configure a database URL and fall back to an in-memory database in development environments.

Finally, we need to initialize Mongoose before using it in our games service. This includes specifying the database URL and waiting for a connection to be established. This happens asynchronously, so can't be part of the games service module definition. We also don't want clients of the games service to have to pass in a Mongoose instance to each function call.

We can address all of these issues by introducing dependency injection to our application. We'll pass in the game service as a dependency to the modules that need it and pass in Mongoose as a dependency to the games service.

 This would also give us the option of writing unit tests for other modules that pass in a test double for the games service itself, so don't use MongoDB at all. In larger applications, this kind of test isolation is important for writing fast and maintainable tests.

# Dependency injection in Node.js

You may have used **dependency injection** (**DI**) frameworks such as Unity, Autofac, NInject, or Spring in .NET or Java. These provide features such as declarative configuration and auto wiring of dependencies. There are similar DI containers available for JavaScript. However, it is more common to pass around dependencies explicitly. JavaScript's module pattern makes this approach more natural than in other languages. We don't need to add a lot of fields and constructors/properties to set up dependencies. We can just wrap modules in an initialization function that takes dependencies as parameters.

In our application, the app module will wire everything together. The application as a whole depends on the database. The games and index routes depend on the game service. To allow the routes to take a dependency on the game service, we just need to top and tail them with a function:

```
'use strict';

module.exports = (gamesService) => {
    var express = require('express');
    var router = express.Router();
    ...
    return router;
};
```

The games service itself is slightly more complicated. We previously added several functions to module.exports, so we need to put these on an object instead. However, this actually results in shorter code. Also, note that we only create the Game schema if it hasn't already been defined, to defend against our exported function being called multiple times:

```
module.exports = (mongoose) => {
    'use strict';
```

```
let Game = mongoose.models['Game'];

if (!Game) {
    const Schema = mongoose.Schema;
    const gameSchema = new Schema({
        word: String,
        setBy: String
    });

    gameSchema.methods.positionsOf = function(character) {
        ...
    };

    Game = mongoose.model('Game', gameSchema);
}

return {
  create: (userId, word) => {
      const game = new Game({
          setBy: userId, word: word.toUpperCase()
      });
      return game.save();
  },
  createdBy: userId => Game.find({setBy: userId}),
  availableTo: userId => Game.where('setBy').ne(userId),
  get: id => Game.findById(id)
};
};
```

Finally, the application itself depends on the database connection and wires up the other dependencies:

```
module.exports = (mongoose) => {
    ...

    let gamesService = require('./services/games')(mongoose);
    let routes = require('./routes/index')(gamesService);
    let games = require('./routes/games')(gamesService);
    ...

    return app;
};
```

# Providing dependencies

We can specify the database URL in an environment variable. When this isn't present, our application will instead make use of an in-memory instance of MongoDB. This will be provided by a library called **Mockgoose**. We install this as a dev dependency, in case we forget to set our environment variable on a production server. We'll get an error rather than quietly using a non-persistent database.

```
> npm install mockgoose@~5.x --save-dev
```

We create a new module under `src/config/mongoose.js` to initialize Mongoose and return a promise that will be fulfilled when it has connected to the database:

```
'use strict';

const mongoose = require('mongoose');
const debug = require('debug')('hangman:config:mongoose');

mongoose.Promise = Promise;
if (!process.env.MONGODB_URL) {
    debug('MongoDB URL not found. Falling back to in-memory
database...');
    require('mockgoose')(mongoose);
}

let db = mongoose.connection;
mongoose.connect(process.env.MONGODB_URL);
module.exports = new Promise(function(resolve, reject) {
    db.once('open', () => resolve(mongoose));
    db.on('error', reject);
});
```

Now we just need to pass this into our application. The following is the code from `bin/www`:

```
...

require('../src/config/mongoose').then((mongoose) => {
    var app = require('../src/app')(mongoose);
    ...
    server.on('listening', onListening);
}).catch(function(error) {
    console.log(error);
    process.exit(1);
});
```

To allow our tests to run, we'll also need to add new `before` functions to make use of this module. The following code is from `test/services/games.js`:

```
'use strict';

const expect = require('chai').expect;

describe('Game service', () => {
  const firstUserId = 'user-id-1';
  const secondUserId = 'user-id-2';

  let service;
  before(done => {
    require('../../src/config/mongoose.js').then((mongoose) => {
      service = require('../../src/services/games.js')(mongoose);
      done();
    }).catch(done);;
  });
  ...
```

The following code is from `test/routes/games.js`:

```
'use strict';

const request = require('supertest');
const expect = require('chai').expect;

describe('/games', () => {
  let agent, userId;
  let mongoose, gamesService, app;

  before(function(done) {
    require('../../src/config/mongoose.js').then((mongoose) => {
      app = require('../../src/app.js')(mongoose);
      gamesService =
        require('../../src/services/games.js')(mongoose);
      done();
    }).catch(done);
  });


  ...
```

We'll also add a global teardown function to close the database connection after all tests have finished. This is just a Mocha `after` hook outside the context of any `describe` block. We add this in a new file under `test/global.js`:

```
'use strict';

after(function(done) {
    require('../src/config/mongoose.js').then(
        (mongoose) => mongoose.disconnect(done));
});
```

Finally, we need to update our `gulpfile.js`, to allow our integration tests to run with the new dependency:

```
gulp.task('integration-test',
        ['lint-integration-test', 'test'], function(done) {
    const TEST_PORT = 5000;

    require('./src/config/mongoose.js').then((mongoose) => {
        let server, teardown = (error) => {
            server.close(() =>
                mongoose.disconnect(() => done(error)));
        };
        server = require('http')
            .createServer(require('./src/app.js')(mongoose))
            .listen(TEST_PORT, function() {
                gulp.src('integration-test/**/*.js')
                    .pipe(
                        ...
                    )
                    .on('error', teardown)
                    .on('end', teardown)
            });
    });
});
```

We can now run our application and tests on a local development machine without needing to have MongoDB running, or we can specify the `MONGO_DB` environment variable if and when we want to use a real MongoDB instance.

# Running database integration tests on Travis CI

We do want to regularly integration test our application against a real MongoDB instance. Fortunately, Travis CI provides various data stores as part of its environment. We just need to tell it that our build requires MongoDB by adding it to our `travis.yml` file. We also need to set the `MONGODB_URL` environment variable for tests to be able to connect to the database:

```
services:
  - mongodb
env:
  global:
    - MONGODB_URL=mongodb://localhost/hangman
```

Now we can run our application as well as our unit and integration tests with a suitable MongoDB instance on development machines and on the CI server.

# Introducing Redis

Redis is often classified as a **key-value** data store. Redis describes itself as a data-structure store. It offers storage types similar to the basic data structures found in most programming languages.

# Why use Redis?

Redis operates entirely in memory, allowing it to be very fast. This, together with its key-value nature, makes it well-suited for use as a cache. It also supports publish/subscribe channels, which allows it to function as a message broker. We'll look at this further in *Chapter 10, Real-time Web Apps in Node.js*.

More generally, Redis can be a useful backend to allow multiple Node.js processes to co-ordinate with one another. Node.js scales horizontally and most websites will run multiple Node.js processes. Many websites have "working" data that doesn't need to be persisted long term, but does need to be available quickly and consistently across all processes. Redis's in-memory nature and range of atomic operations make it very useful for this purpose.

Redis is built more for speed than durability. There are various options to configure it, but all expect some amount of data loss in the event of an outage. This is a compromise of Redis working entirely in-memory for speed. It is possible to reduce data loss to no more than the last second of writes before an outage, without significantly compromising on speed. Redis can be configured to completely minimize data loss by syncing to disk after each operation. However, this has a more significant impact on performance and negates the advantages of Redis's in-memory nature.

# Installing Redis

Source distributions of Redis are available from `http://redis.io/download`.

For Windows, it is more useful to download a pre-built binary. It is available as a signed package via NuGet and Chocolatey. If you have Chocolatey available, you can install Redis by running the following command:

```
> choco install redis-64
```

Alternatively, you can download an unsigned version of the installer from `https://github.com/MSOpenTech/redis/releases`

Once installed, you can start Redis by running `redis-server`. In a separate window, run `redis-cli` to connect to the server and run commands.

# Using Redis as a key-value store

Everything in Redis is stored against a key. Keys in Redis can be any binary data, but it's best to think of them as strings. Various types of value can be stored against each key.

Redis refers to simple scalar values as **Strings**. Redis also has special treatment for scalar integers. The following example sets and updates a key named `counter`:

```
127.0.0.1:6379> set counter 100
OK
127.0.0.1:6379> get counter
"100"
127.0.0.1:6379> incr counter
(integer) 101
```

This increment operation is atomic. Redis also supports setting values atomically. The following command will fail because the key already exists:

```
127.0.0.1:6379> set counter 200 nx
(nil)
```

These features can help coordinating between servers. Redis also supports setting expiry times for keys. This makes it possible to offer caching behavior similar to memcache. Redis has even more flexibility, though, as we'll see in the next section.

# Storing structured data in Redis

In addition to simple key-value pairs, Redis supports other more structured data types.

**Lists** are ordered collections of values. They are stored as a linked list rather than as arrays. This makes adding/removing elements at the ends of the list efficient (at the cost of slower retrieval of items from the list by index), for example:

```
127.0.0.1:6379> rpush fruit apple banana pear
(integer) 3
127.0.0.1:6379> rpop fruit
"pear"
127.0.0.1:6379> lpush fruit orange
(integer) 3
127.0.0.1:6379> lrange fruit 0 -1
1) "orange"
2) "apple"
3) "banana"
```

Note that lrange takes start and end indices. Negative values count backwards from the end of the list, so -1 refers to the last element. Being able to push/pop from either end of a list means that they can be used as stacks or queues, for example, for allowing processes to communicate in a producer-consumer arrangement.

**Hashes** are a set of field-value pairs. These are not as rich as MongoDB documents, but allow us to associate some data together. For example, we could have implemented our game service using Redis:

```
127.0.0.1:6379> hmset game:2 word JavaScript setBy user-id-7
OK
127.0.0.1:6379> hget game:2 word
"JavaScript"
127.0.0.1:6379> hgetall game:2
1) "word"
2) "JavaScript"
3) "setBy"
4) "user-id-7"
```

Note that the top-level key `game:2` here is just a convention. It can be useful for developers to namespace keys in this way, but Redis only understands them as strings.

**Sets** are unordered collections of values, for example:

```
127.0.0.1:6379> sadd numbers one two three
(integer) 3
127.0.0.1:6379> smembers numbers
1) "two"
2) "three"
3) "one"
```

Sets support mathematical operations such as unions and intersections. They also support the retrieval (with optional atomic removal) of random elements.

**Sorted sets** are collections of values, each associated with a numerical score:

```
127.0.0.1:6379> zadd votes 3 Aye
(integer) 1
127.0.0.1:6379> zadd votes 4 No
(integer) 1
127.0.0.1:6379> zadd votes 1 Abstain
(integer) 1
127.0.0.1:6379> zrevrange votes 0 1
1) "No"
2) "Aye"
```

Note that the ranges are ordered smallest to largest by default. We request a reverse range above to get the element with the highest score first. Sorted sets are useful for implementing voting systems (as previously shown) or ranking systems.

# Building a user ranking system with Redis

We want to be able to rank users based on how many games they have completed. We will create a user service, implemented in Redis, that provides the following functionality:

- Record when a user successfully completes a game
- Return the top three users across the site
- Return the rank of a given user

We will first add a feature to make the site a bit more user-friendly by allowing users to choose a screen name.

# Using Redis from Node.js

First, we'll need to install a Node.js client library for Redis. We'll also use the promise library Bluebird to convert the Redis client library to promises:

```
> npm install redis --save
> npm install bluebird --save
```

First, we'll create a module for configuring the Redis client as shown here in `src/config/redis.js`:

```
'use strict';

const bluebird = require('bluebird');
const redis = require('redis');
bluebird.promisifyAll(redis.RedisClient.prototype);
module.exports = redis.createClient(process.env.REDIS_URL);
```

Now we can create a new user service with methods for getting and setting a username, in `src/services/users.js`:

```
'use strict';

let redisClient = require('../config/redis.js');

module.exports = {
    getUsername: userId =>
        redisClient.getAsync(`user:${userId}:name`),
    setUsername: (userId, name) =>
        redisClient.setAsync(`user:${userId}:name`, name)
};
```

Note that the Redis client provides functions for each Redis command (such as `get` and `set`). Bluebird provides promise-based versions of each function suffixed with `Async`.

Of course, now that we have test infrastructure for our project, we should add tests for new code as we go as shown here `test/services/users.js`:

```
'use strict';

const expect = require('chai').expect;
const service = require('../../src/services/users.js');
```

```
describe('User service', function() {
    describe('getUsername', function() {
        it('should return a previously set username', done => {
            const userId = 'user-id-1';
            const name = 'User Name';
            service.setUsername(userId, name)
                .then(() => service.getUsername(userId))
                .then(actual => expect(actual).to.equal(name))
                .then(() => done(), done);
        });

        it('should return null if no username is set', done => {
            const userId = 'user-id-2';

            service.getUsername(userId)
                .then(name => expect(name).to.be.null)
                .then(() => done(), done);
        });
    });
});
```

# Testing with redis-js

As with the tests for our games service, we want to be able to integrate with a Redis instance on our CI server. But we don't want to introduce any new dependencies for development. This time, we will make use of a library called redis-js for local testing. Unlike Mockgoose, this does not use an in-memory version of the real DB engine (Redis is already in-memory). This is instead a re-implementation of the Node.js Redis client that stores all of its data in-process:

```
> npm install redis-js --save-dev
```

Now we can create a module for obtaining the environment-appropriate Redis reference as shown here src/config/redis.js:

```
'use strict';

const bluebird = require('bluebird');
const debug = require('debug')('hangman:config:redis');

if (process.env.REDIS_URL) {
    let redis = require('redis');
    bluebird.promisifyAll(redis.RedisClient.prototype);
    module.exports = redis.createClient(process.env.REDIS_URL);
} else {
```

```
        debug('Redis URL not found. Falling back to mock DB...');
        let redisClient = require('redis-js');
        bluebird.promisifyAll(redisClient);
        module.exports = redisClient;
}
```

Note that, unlike Mongoose, the Node.js Redis client can be used immediately. Any commands issued before it has connected are actually queued up internally. This means we can just return the client from the module and require it directly. There wouldn't be any benefit in this case to the dependency injection we used with Mongoose.

We also need to add Redis to our `.travis.yml` file so it runs on the CI server:

```
services:
  - mongodb
  - redis-server
env:
  global:
    - MONGODB_URL=mongodb://localhost/hangman
    - REDIS_URL=redis://127.0.0.1:6379/
```

Finally, we need to close the client once our tests have completed, as we did with Mongoose. We also ensure we empty the database on startup (as we don't have a way of deleting user data via the service interface, as we do with games). The following code is from `test/global.js`:

```
'use strict';

before(function(done) {
    require('../src/config/redis.js').flushdbAsync().then(() =>
done());
});

after(function(done) {
    require('../src/config/redis.js').quit();
    require('../src/config/mongoose.js').then(
        (mongoose) => mongoose.disconnect(done));
});
```

The following code is from `gulpfile.js`:

```
        let server, teardown = (error) => {
            require('./src/config/redis.js').quit();
            server.close(() =>
                mongoose.disconnect(() => done(error)));
        };
```

# Implementing user rankings with Redis

Now we are ready to add the user ranking functionality to our service. The following code is from `src/services/users.js`:

```
module.exports = {
  ...

  recordWin: userId =>
    redisClient.zincrbyAsync('user:wins', 1, userId),

  getTopPlayers: () =>
    redisClient.zrevrangeAsync('user:wins', 0, 2, 'withscores')
    .then(interleaved => {
      if (interleaved.length === 0) {
        return [];
      }
      let userIds = interleaved
        .filter((user, index) => index % 2 === 0)
        .map((userId) => `user:${userId}:name`);
      return redisClient.mgetAsync(userIds)
        .then(names => names.map((username, index) => ({
          name: username,
          userId: interleaved[index * 2],
          wins: parseInt(interleaved[index * 2 + 1], 10)
        })));
    }),

  getRanking: userId => {
    return Promise.all([
      redisClient.zrevrankAsync('user:wins', userId),
      redisClient.zscoreAsync('user:wins', userId)
    ]).then(out => {
      if (out[0] === null) {
        return null;
      }
      return { rank: out[0] + 1, wins: parseInt(out[1], 10) };
    });
  }
};
```

Most of the Redis commands used here will be familiar from earlier in the chapter. The most interesting function is `getTopPlayers`. This makes use of `zrevrange` with the `withscores` option. This returns an array of user IDs and scores (interleaved together). We make a second request to the database using `mget` (multivalued get) to retrieve the names of all the users. Once this returns we can combine all the data for each user together into an object.

## Making use of the users service

Wiring this functionality up to the rest of our application doesn't use any techniques we haven't seen before, so is omitted from the printed code listings for brevity. The full implementation can be found in the companion code for this chapter, along with tests for the rest of the user service methods, at `https://github.com/NodeJsForDevelopers/chapter09`.

# A note on security

We have been running MongoDB and Redis with their default out-of-the-box settings. This is fine for development purposes. Deploying these services into production requires additional consideration around security. You can find more resources on this at `https://docs.mongodb.com/manual/administration/security-checklist/` and `http://redis.io/topics/security`.

# Summary

In this chapter, we have understood the difference between different types of database and learned about the key features of MongoDB and Redis. We also persisted our application's data using these databases and used dependency injection to make our application more flexible. We also learned how to configure our development and integration environments to use appropriate database instances.

Persistence may be considered the bottom layer of our system. In the next chapter, we'll introduce real-time client/server communication into our application. This frontend functionality means focusing more on the top layer of our system. However, we'll also see Redis playing an important role in supporting this functionality.

# 10
# Creating Real-time Web Apps

The web has offered an ever more dynamic and interactive user experience. Throughout the 90s, most of the web consisted of static pages or server-side rendered pages. Frames and iframes made it possible to reload parts of the page in a limited way. When Ajax appeared in the mid-2000s, it allowed pages to be much more engaging. Client-side JavaScript could now request data from the server on demand and update the page dynamically.

Real-time web applications are the next step in this evolution. These are applications where the server pushes data to clients without the clients needing to initiate a request. This allows a user to be notified of new information or for users to interact with each other in real time.

In this chapter, we will cover the following topics:

- Establishing a two-way communication channel between the client and server
- Adding real-time interactivity to our application
- Introducing a backend to scale our real-time application across multiple servers

## Understanding options for real-time communication

Real-time web applications need a bidirectional communication channel between the client and the server. This is any persistent connection that allows the server to push additional data to the client when needed. The WebSockets protocol is the modern standard for this kind of communication and is implemented by most browsers.

WebSocket connections are initiated via HTTP, but otherwise do not depend on it. The WebSocket protocol defines a way of sending messages bi-directionally over a TCP connection. TCP is the low-level transport protocol that usually underlies HTTP. WebSockets are still a relatively new technology and not fully supported by all clients and servers. Most modern web browsers today do support WebSockets. However, intermediate servers (proxies, firewalls, and load-balancers) can prevent WebSocket connections from working (either through lack of support or intentionally blocking non-HTTP traffic). In these cases, there are alternative ways of achieving real-time communication.

The EventSource standard defines a way for a server to send events to clients over HTTP and defines a JavaScript API for handling these events. It is not as efficient or widely-supported as WebSockets, but is better supported by some older servers and clients.

The ultimate fallback is **long-polling**. This is when the client initiates an ordinary (Ajax) request to the server, which stays open until the server has some data to send. As soon as the client receives any data, it makes another request to the server for the next message. This introduces additional bandwidth overheads and latency compared to WebSockets, but has the widest support as it just uses ordinary HTTP requests.

Ideally, a client and server can negotiate to work out the best available type of connection to use. This can be quite a complicated process, though. Fortunately, there are libraries which can handle this for us.

# Introducing Socket.IO

Socket.IO is a mature and well-established library with excellent cross-browser support. It aims to quickly and reliably establish a bidirectional communication channel in a cross-browser compatible way. It provides a consistent abstraction, based on idiomatic JavaScript events, for real-time communication between the client and the server over this channel. If you have ever used SignalR in .NET, you can think of Socket.IO as the JavaScript equivalent.

# Implementing a chat room with Socket.IO

Let's implement a chat lobby for users of our application to talk to one another. First, we need to install Socket.IO:

```
> npm install --save socket.io
```

The server-side implementation for this is very simple. We just need to tell Socket.IO that, whenever a user sends a chat message, we want to broadcast this to all connected users as given here `src/realtime/chat.js`:

```
'use strict';

module.exports = io => {
    io.on('connection', (socket) => {
        socket.on('chatMessage', (message) => {
            io.emit('chatMessage', message);
        });
    });
};
```

Here, we add a listener to Socket.IO's `connection` event. Our listener is fired whenever a new client connects to the application. The `socket` variable represents the connection to that specific client.

The `io` parameter shown previously will be a Socket.IO instance. To create one of these, we need to provide a reference to the HTTP server that will host our application, so that Socket.IO can add its own connection handling. To keep things tidier, we'll add a new `server` module in `src/server.js` to set up our server, start our Express application, and initialize Socket.IO:

```
'use strict';

module.exports = require('./config/mongoose').then(mongoose => {
    const app = require('../src/app')(mongoose);
    const server = require('http').createServer(app);
    const io = require('socket.io')(server);
    require('./realtime/chat')(io);

    server.on('close', () => {
        require('../src/config/redis.js').quit();
        mongoose.disconnect();
    });
    return server;
});
```

This also allows us to simplify the bootstrap script and our integration tests as in bin/www:

```
#!/usr/bin/env node

var debug = require('debug')('hangman:server');
var port = normalizePort(process.env.PORT || '3000');
```

```
require('../src/server').then((server) => {
    server.listen(port);
    server.on('error', onError);
    server.on('listening', onListening.bind(server));
}).catch(function(error) {
    debug(error);
    process.exit(1);
});

...

function onListening() {
  var addr = this.address();
  ...
}
```

... and in `gulpfile.js`:

```
gulp.task('integration-test',
        ['lint-integration-test', 'test'], done => {
  const TEST_PORT = 5000;

  require('./src/server.js').then((server) => {
    server.listen(TEST_PORT);
    server.on('listening', () => {
      gulp.src('integration-test/**/*.js')
        .pipe(
          ...
        }))
        .on('error', error => server.close(() => done(error)))
        .on('end', () => server.close(done))
    });
  });
});
```

Now we need to add the client-side code to communicate with this service. First, we'll add a place for our chat lobby to the application home page as given here `src/views/index.hjs`:

```
{{/topPlayers}}
</ol>
<hr/>
<h3>Lobby</h3>
<form class="chat">
  <div id="messages"></div>
```

```
        <input id="message"/><input type="submit" value="Send"/>
    </form>
  </body>
</html>
```

Now, we'll create the client-side script to connect this with the server as given here `src/public/scripts/chat.js`:

```
$(document).ready(function() {
    'use strict';
    var socket = io();

    $('form.chat').submit(function(event){
        socket.emit('chatMessage', $('#message').val());
        $('#message').val('');
        event.preventDefault();
    });

    socket.on('chatMessage', function(message){
        $('#messages').append($('<p>').text(message));
    });
});
```

Finally, we need to include our new script in the page and include the Socket.IO client-side script that defines the preceding `io` function `src/view/index.hjs`:

```
<!DOCTYPE html>
<html>
  <head>
    <title>{{ title }}</title>
    <link rel="stylesheet" href="/stylesheets/style.css" />
    ...
    <script src="/scripts/index.js"></script>
    <script src="/socket.io/socket.io.js"></script>
    <script src="/scripts/chat.js"></script>
  </head>
  <body>
    ...
```

Note that we haven't created the `socket.io.js` script anywhere. This is served as a result of attaching Socket.IO to our server in `src/server.js`. Since we don't define the `io` variable in our own script, we need to let ESLint know that it exists as a global variable as given in `gulpfile.js`:

```
gulp.task('lint-client', function() {
    return gulp.src('src/public/**/*.js')
```

```
                .pipe(eslint({ envs: [ 'browser', 'jquery' ],
                        globals: { io: false } }))
                .pipe(eslint.format())
                .pipe(eslint.failAfterError());
    });
```

Now, if we open up our application in two browser windows, they can send chat messages to each other!

# Scaling real-time Node.js applications

Since our chat messages are being relayed via the server, clients can currently only communicate with other clients connected to the same server. This is a problem if we want to scale our application horizontally across many servers.

This is easy to fix, but tricky to demonstrate. To do so, we need to have two separate instances of our application running. This will be more realistic and more useful if they are also using the same shared databases for persistence. So we need to start up MongoDB and Redis, then start two instances of our application on different ports (so that they don't collide).

This means running all of the following commands (replacing the dbpath of MongoDB as appropriate for your setup):

```
> redis-server
> mongod --dbpath C:\data\mongodb
> set MONGODB_URL=mongodb://localhost/hangman
> set REDIS_URL=redis://127.0.0.1:6379/
> set PORT=3000
> npm start
> set PORT=3001
> npm start
```

The commands that start the database or application servers also occupy the current console. So, to be able to run all of these commands, we need to execute them in separate windows or tell them to execute in the background. On Windows, this can be achieved with the following batch script:

```
@echo off
START /B redis-server
START /B mongod --dbpath C:\data\mongodb
set MONGODB_URL=mongodb://localhost/hangman
set REDIS_URL=redis://127.0.0.1:6379/
SLEEP 2
```

```
set PORT=3000
START /B npm start
SLEEP 1
set PORT=3001
START /B npm start
```

Now you can connect separate browsers to a separate application instance at `http://localhost:3000` and `http://localhost:3001`. Notice that two clients connected to the same application instance can receive messages from each other, but not from clients on the other application instance.

To resolve this, we need a shared backend through which all the applications can communicate. Redis is a perfect candidate for this.

# Using Redis as a backend

Socket.IO makes use of the **adapter** pattern to support different backends. An adapter is just a wrapper for converting one interface into another. Socket.IO has a standard backend interface and various adapters to allow different implementations to work with this interface. By default, it uses an in-memory adapter that is limited to a single process. However, the Socket.IO project also provides an adaptor for using Redis as a backend:

```
> npm install socket.io-redis --save
```

Once installed, using this is simply a matter of telling Socket.IO where to find our Redis instance (we skip this in test environments where we only have one application process) as given here `src/server.js`:

```javascript
'use strict';

module.exports = require('./config/mongoose').then(mongoose => {
    const app = require('../src/app')(mongoose);
    const server = require('http').createServer(app);
    const io = require('socket.io')(server);

    if (process.env.REDIS_URL && process.env.NODE_ENV !== 'test') {
        const redisAdapter = require('socket.io-redis');
        io.adapter(redisAdapter(process.env.REDIS_URL));
    }

    require('./realtime/chat')(io);

    ...
    return server;
});
```

And that's it! We don't require any other changes to our code to support scalability. If you restart your application instances now, you should find that clients can communicate between them.

# Integrating Socket.IO with Express

So far, apart from sharing the same server, the Socket.IO and Express parts of our application are completely independent. While it's good that they are loosely coupled, some cross-cutting concerns may be relevant to both.

For example, both parts of our application should have a mutually consistent way of identifying the current user. This is especially important if they are to come together to provide a single coherent user experience.

First, let's extend our user middleware to provide the current user's name as well as their ID, by looking them up in the user service as given here `src/middleware/users.js`:

```
'use strict';

module.exports = (service) => {
    const uuid = require('uuid');

    return function(req, res, next) {
        let userId = req.cookies.userId;
        if (!userId) {
            userId = uuid.v4();
            res.cookie('userId', userId);
            req.user = {
                id: userId
            };
            next();
        } else {
            service.getUsername(userId).then(username => {
                req.user = {
                    id: userId,
                    name: username
                };
                next();
            });
        }
    };
};
```

You can find updated tests for this middleware in the book's companion code.

This will mean injecting our user service as a dependency, like we do for the other middleware modules (that is, routes) in our application as given in `src/app.js`:

```
...

let gamesService = require('./service/games')(mongoose);
let usersService = require('./service/users');

let users = require('./middleware/users')(usersService);
let routes = require('./routes/index')(gamesService, usersService);
let games = require('./routes/games')(gamesService, usersService);
let profile = require('./routes/profile')(usersService);
...
```

The interesting part is allowing Socket.IO to make use of this middleware. Socket.IO has its own concept of middleware very similar to that of Express. Recall that Express middleware functions take parameters for the current request, response, and a `next` callback. Socket.IO middleware functions just take a communication socket and a `next` callback. However, we can access the original HTTP handshake that initiated the socket. This allows us to adapt our Express middleware to Socket.IO middleware and use it as follows, in `src/server.js`:

```
'use strict';

module.exports = require('./config/mongoose').then(mongoose => {
    let app = require('../src/app')(mongoose);
    let server = require('http').createServer(app);
    let io = require('socket.io')(server);

    if (process.env.REDIS_URL) {
        let redisAdapter = require('socket.io-redis');
        io.adapter(redisAdapter(process.env.REDIS_URL));
    }

    io.use(adapt(require('cookie-parser')()));
    const usersService = require('./services/users.js');
    io.use(adapt(require('./middleware/users')(usersService)));

    require('./realtime/chat')(io);

    ...
```

```
        return server;
    });

    function adapt(expressMiddleware) {
        return (socket, next) => {
            expressMiddleware(socket.request, socket.request.res, next);
        };
    }
```

Now the user middleware will run for Socket.IO as well as regular HTTP requests, making user data available to Socket.IO as well. Let's use this to include usernames in our chat. First, we need to update our server as given in `src/realtime/chat.js`:

```
    'use strict';

    module.exports = io => {
        io.on('connection', (socket) => {
            socket.on('chatMessage', (message) => {
                io.emit('chatMessage', {
                    username: socket.request.user.name,
                    message: message
                });
            });
        });
    }
```

Notice that Socket.IO allows us to send objects instead of simple strings as the event payload. Now we just need to make use of this in the client as given here `src/public/scripts/chat.js`:

```
    $(document).ready(function() {
        'use strict';

        var socket = io();
        ...
        socket.on('chatMessage', function(data){
            $('#messages').append(
                $('<p>').text(data.message)
                    .prepend($('<b>').text(data.username)));
        });
    });
```

If you now open the application in separate browser sessions and specify different usernames, you will see these in the chat output.

# Directing Socket.IO messages

Now that we have access to usernames, we can also announce the arrival of users in the lobby. We can do this by extending our Socket.IO connection event handler as given here `src/realtime/chat.js`:

```
'use strict';

module.exports = io => {

    io.on('connection', (socket) => {
        const username = socket.request.user.name;

        if(username) {
            socket.broadcast.emit('chatMessage', {
                username: username,
                message: 'has arrived',
                type: 'action'
            });
        }

        socket.on('chatMessage', (message) => {
            io.emit('chatMessage', {
                username: username,
                message: message
            });
        });
    });
}
```

Here, we use `socket.broadcast.emit`, rather than `io.emit`, to send the event to all clients except for the current socket. Note that we also add extra data to the message. This time we add a `type` field (set to `'action'` for the arrival message) to allow different visual presentation of different types of message. We can achieve this by updating our client-side code to set additional CSS classes based on the message type as given here `src/public/scripts/chat.js`:

```
socket.on('chatMessage', function(data){
    $('#messages').append(
        $('<p>').text(data.message).addClass(data.type)
            .prepend($('<b>').text(data.username)));
});
```

 You can find the CSS file for the example application in the companion code.

Let's also enforce that users have to choose a username before they can take part in the chat as given here `src/realtime/chat.js`:

```
'use strict';

module.exports = io => {
    io.on('connection', (socket) => {
        ...
        socket.on('chatMessage', (message) => {
            if (!username) {
                socket.emit('chatMessage', {
                    message: 'Please choose a username',
                    type: 'warning'
                });
            } else {
                io.emit('chatMessage', {
                    username: username,
                    message: message
                });
            }
        });
    });
}
```

Here, we use `socket.emit` rather than `io.emit` to send a message to the client associated with the current socket.

# Testing Socket.IO applications

Now let's look at how we can test our chat module. To talk to it from our tests we'll need a Socket.IO client. The Socket.IO project provides another package for this:

```
> npm install socket.io-client --save-dev
```

The infrastructure for our tests consists of setting up a server and multiple clients as given here `test/realtime/chat.js`:

```
'use strict';
describe('chat', function() {
    const expect = require('chai').expect;
    let server, io, url, createUser, createdClients = [];

    beforeEach(done => {
        server = require('http').createServer();
```

```
            server.listen((err) => {
                if (err) {
                    done(err);
                } else {
                    const addr = server.address();
                    url = 'http://localhost:' + addr.port + '/chat';

                    io = require('socket.io')(server);
                    require('../../src/realtime/chat.js')(io);

                    done();
                }
            });
        });

        afterEach(done => {
            createdClients.forEach(client => client.disconnect());
            server.close(done);
        });

        const createClient = require('socket.io-client');
        createUser = (name, room) => {
            let user = {
                name: name,
                client: createClient(url)
            };
            createdClients.push(user.client);

            return user;
        };
    });
```

Here, we create an HTTP server without specifying an address, so that the OS will assign us an available port. We then use this this server to host our chat implementation.

Since we're running the chat module in isolation, we don't have our users middleware available, so will need an alternative way to provide usernames. We can do this with a stub middleware in our tests that reads usernames directly from a header:

```
'use strict';

describe('chat', function() {
    const expect = require('chai').expect;
    let server, io, url, createUser, createdClients = [];

    beforeEach(done => {
```

```
server = require('http').createServer();

server.listen((err) => {
    if (err) {
        done(err);
    } else {
        const addr = server.address();
        url = 'http://localhost:' + addr.port;

        io = require('socket.io')(server);
        io.use((socket, next) => {
            socket.request.user = {
                name: socket.request.headers.username
            };
            next();
        });

        require('../../src/realtime/chat.js')(io);

        done();
    }
});
});

...

const createClient = require('socket.io-client');
createUser = (name, room) => {
    let headers = {};
    if (name) {
        headers.username = name;
    }

    let user = {
        name: name,
        client: createClient(url, { extraHeaders: headers})
    };
    createdClients.push(user.client);
    user.client.emit('joinRoom', room);

    return user;
};
});
```

Now we are ready to implement our tests. The first two, for messages initiated from the server, are quite simple:

```
it('warns unnamed users to choose a username', done => {
    let unnamedUser = createUser();
    unnamedUser.client.emit('chatMessage', 'Hello!');
    unnamedUser.client.on('chatMessage', (data) => {
        expect(data.message).to.contain('choose a username');
        expect(data.username).to.be.undefined;
        expect(data.type).to.equal('warning');
        done();
    });
});

it('broadcasts arrival of named users', done => {
    let connectedUser = createUser();
    let newUser = createUser('User1');
    connectedUser.client.on('chatMessage', (data) => {
        expect(data.message).to.contain('arrived');
        expect(data.username).to.equal(newUser.name);
        expect(data.type).to.equal('action');
        done();
    });
});
```

Testing messages sent between clients requires a little more care to capture each client's receipt of the message:

```
it('emits messages from named users back to all users', done => {
    let namedUser = createUser('User1');
    let otherUser = createUser();
    let messageReceived = function(data) {
        this.received = data;

        if (namedUser.received && otherUser.received) {

            [namedUser.received, otherUser.received]
            .forEach(received => {
                expect(received.message).to.equal('Hello!');
                expect(received.username)
                    .to.equal(namedUser.name);
            });
            done();
        }
    };
```

```
        otherUser.client.on('chatMessage',
                              messageReceived.bind(otherUser));
        namedUser.client.on('chatMessage',
                              messageReceived.bind(namedUser));
        namedUser.client.emit('chatMessage', 'Hello!');
    });
```

# Organizing Socket.IO applications

Now that we have a chat lobby on the index page of our application, it's a bit odd that users have to reload the page (and lose the chat history) to find out about new games. We can use Socket.IO to update these as well.

## Exposing real-time updates to the model

First, we'll need our games service itself to expose events for when games are added or removed. Here we use the Mongoose-provided `post` method to hook into persistence operations on games as given here `src/services/games.js`:

```
'use strict';

const EventEmitter = require('events');
const emitter = new EventEmitter();

module.exports = (mongoose) => {
    let Game = mongoose.models['Game'];

    if (!Game) {
        let Schema = mongoose.Schema;
        let gameSchema = new Schema({
            word: String,
            setBy: String
        });

        ...

        gameSchema.post('save', game =>
            emitter.emit('gameSaved', game));
        gameSchema.post('remove', game =>
            emitter.emit('gameRemoved', game));

        Game = mongoose.model('Game', gameSchema);
    }
```

```
    return {
        ...
        get: id => Game.findById(id),
        events: emitter
    };
};

module.exports.events = emitter;
```

We expose an **event emitter** to allow other modules to subscribe to events for when games are added or removed. Event emitters are a built-in feature of Node.js, which provide a simple way to expose custom events. Note that the Mongoose `Schema` class is itself an event emitter, so we could just expose this directly. However, this would be leaking details about the implementation of our games service.

 Again, you can find new tests for these changes in the companion code.

# Organizing Socket.IO applications using namespaces

Real-time chat and real-time updates to the list of games are quite distinct functional areas of our application. Socket.IO provides **namespaces** to allow us to organise events. This allows us to still use a single connection between the client and the server, without having to worry about clashing event names between different functional areas. This is very useful as applications become larger and more complex.

Putting our chat functionality under a namespace is a very simple change on the client and the server (and in our tests).

The following code is from `src/public/scripts/chat.js`:

```
$(document).ready(function() {
    'use strict';
    var socket = io('/chat');
    ...
```

The following code is from `src/realtime/chat.js`:

```
'use strict';

module.exports = io => {
    const namespace = io.of('/chat');
```

```
namespace.on('connection', (socket) => {
    ...

    socket.on('chatMessage', (message) => {
        if (!username) {
            ...
        } else {
            namespace.emit('chatMessage', {
                username: username,
                message: message
            });
        }
    });
});
};
```

The following code is from `test/realtime/chat.js`:

```
const addr = server.address();
url = 'http://localhost:' + addr.port + '/chat';
```

Now we can add a new Socket.IO module for exposing changes to games. This simply needs to forward events from our games service to connected Socket.IO clients.

We add the following code under `src/realtime/games.js`:

```
'use strict';

module.exports = (io, service) => {
    io.of('/games').on('connection', (socket) => {
        forwardEvent('gameSaved', socket);
        forwardEvent('gameRemoved', socket);
    });

    function forwardEvent(name, socket) {
        service.events.on(name, game => {
            if (game.setBy !== socket.request.user.id) {
                socket.emit(name, game.id);
            }
        });
    }
};
```

We also need to include this module in the initialisation of our server.

The following code is from `src/server.js`:

```
'use strict';

module.exports = require('./config/mongoose').then(mongoose => {
    ...

    require('./realtime/chat')(io);
    const gamesService = require('./services/games.js')(mongoose);
    require('./realtime/games')(io, gamesService);

    ...
    return server;
});
```

The corresponding client just needs to connect to the `/games` namespace and update the list accordingly.

The following code is from `src/public/scripts/index.js`:

```
var socket = io('/games');
var availableGames = $('#availableGames');

socket.on('gameSaved', function(game) {
    availableGames.append(
        '<li id="' + game + '"><a href="/games/' + game + '">' +
            game + '</a></li>');
});
socket.on('gameRemoved', function(game) {
    $('#' + game).remove();
});
```

The following code is added to `src/views/index.hjs`:

```
<h3>Games available to play</h3>
<ul id="availableGames">
  {{#availableGames}}
    <li id="{{id}}"><a href="/games/{{id}}">{{id}}</a></li>
  {{/availableGames}}
</ul>
```

 In practice, it would better to use a client-side MV* library such as Knockout or Backbone to update the page based on model changes, rather than manipulating the DOM like this, but that's outside the scope of this book.

Now, if you open the application in two separate browser sessions and create a new game in one browser window, it will immediately appear in the other.

# Partitioning Socket.IO clients using rooms

The final piece of functionality we're going to add in this chapter is the ability for users playing the same game to talk to one another. We can re-use the chat functionality we've already written for this. However, we want a separate chat for the lobby on the homepage and for each game.

Socket.IO provides **rooms** for directing messages to different groups of clients. Remember that namespaces allow us to divide our application into different functional areas. Rooms allow us to divide up clients within the same functional area.

Rooms in Socket.IO are just string identifiers and we add clients to a room using the `socket.join` function. We'll introduce a new `joinRoom` event to allow our clients to ask our server to add them to a particular room. We'll respond to this event on the server as follows:

The following code is from `src/realtime/chat.js`:

```
'use strict';

module.exports = io => {
    const namespace = io.of('/chat');

    namespace.on('connection', (socket) => {
        const username = socket.request.user.name;

        socket.on('joinRoom', (room) => {
            socket.join(room);
            if (username) {
                socket.broadcast.to(room).emit('chatMessage', {
                    username: username,
                    message: 'has arrived',
                    type: 'action'
                });
            }

            socket.on('chatMessage', (message) => {
                if (!username) {
                    ...
                } else {
                    namespace.to(room).emit('chatMessage', {
                        username: username,
                        message: message
```

```
                          });
                      }
                  });

              socket.on('disconnect', () => {
                  if (username) {
                      socket.broadcast.to(room).emit('chatMessage', {
                          username: username,
                          message: 'has left',
                          type: 'action'
                      });
                  }
              });
          });
      });
  };
```

Note that we also announce when users leave a particular room, in the same way that we announce arrivals. Again, you can find the additional test for this functionality in the example code.

We'll add the chat functionality into the game page and specify the correct room using a data attribute on the chat form.

The following code is from `src/views/game.hjs`:

```
<!DOCTYPE html>
<html>
  <head>
    <title>Hangman - Game #{{id}}</title>
    <link rel="stylesheet" href="/stylesheets/style.css" />
    <script src="https://cdnjs.cloudflare.com/ajax/libs/jquery/2.1.4/
jquery.min.js"></script>
    <script src="/scripts/game.js"></script>
    <script src="/socket.io/socket.io.js"></script>
    <script src="/scripts/chat.js"></script>
    <base href="/games/{{ id }}/">
  </head>
  <body>
    <h1>Hangman - Game #{{id}}</h1>
    <h2 id="word" data-length="{{ length }}"></h2>
    <p>Press letter keys to guess</p>
    <h3>Missed letters:</h3>
    <p id="missedLetters"></p>

    <hr/>
```

```
    <h3>Discussion</h3>
    <form class="chat" data-room="{{id}}">
      <div id="messages"></div>
      <input id="message"/><input type="submit" value="Send"/>
    </form>
  </body>
</html>
```

The following code is from `src/views/index.hjs`:

```
<hr/>
<h3>Lobby</h3>
<form class="chat" data-room="lobby">
  <div id="messages"></div>
  <input id="message"/><input type="submit" value="Send"/>
</form>
```

Then we need to update the client script to join the correct room when connecting.

The following code is from `src/public/scripts/chat.js`:

```
$(document).ready(function() {
    'use strict';

    var chat = $('form.chat');
    var socket = io('/chat');

    socket.emit('joinRoom', chat.data('room'));
    chat.submit(function(event){
        ...
    });
    ...
});
```

Finally, we need to make sure that typing a chat message doesn't interfere with playing the game. We can do this by only treating keypresses as guesses for the game when the user isn't typing in the chat message box.

The following code is from `src/public/javascript/game.js`:

```
$(document).keydown(function(event) {
    if (!$('.chat #message').is(':focus') &&
            event.which >= 65 && event.which <= 90) {
        var letter = String.fromCharCode(event.which);
        if (guessedLetters.indexOf(letter) === -1) {
            guessedLetters.push(letter);
```

```
                    guessLetter(letter);
                }
            }
        });
```

 You can find new and updated tests for this functionality in
the companion code.

Putting this all together, we can now have multiple clients talking to one another in separate rooms:

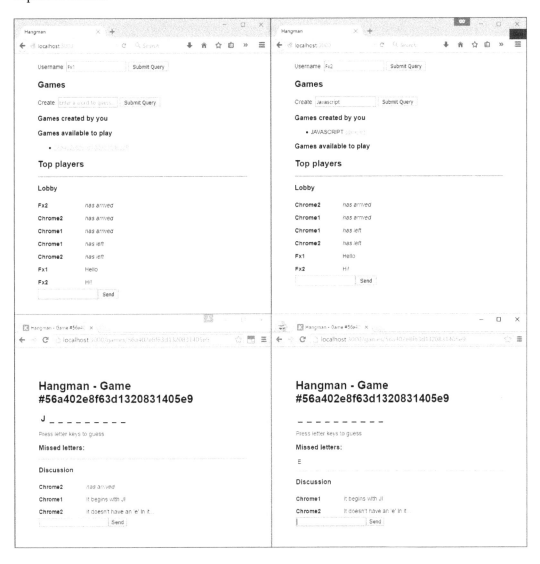

# Summary

In this chapter, we have created a real-time client/server communication channel using Socket.IO, used Redis as a backend to scale a real-time application horizontally, integrated Socket.IO with Express middleware, and organized our application using Socket.IO namespaces and rooms.

As the network connectivity of our application is becoming more complicated, it's more important to test the application on a web server outside of the development or CI environment. In the next chapter, we'll look at how to deploy our application to the web.

# 11
# Deploying Node.js Applications

So far, we have only run our application in our local development environment. In this chapter, we will deploy it to the Web. There are many different options for hosting an application. We will work through one deployment option to quickly get an application up and running. We will also discuss broader principles and alternative options for deploying Node.js applications.

In this chapter, we will cover the following topics:

- Deploying our application to the Web
- Using application logs to diagnose issues on remote servers
- Setting up database servers and environmental configuration
- Deploying automatically from Travis CI

 If you want to follow along with this chapter, you can use the code from `https://github.com/NodeJsForDevelopers/chapter10/` as a starting point. This contains the example code from the end of *Chapter 10, Creating Real-time Web Apps*, which we will build on in this chapter.

# Working with Heroku

**Heroku** is a cloud-based platform for web applications. It aims to allow developers to focus on applications rather than infrastructure. It provides a low-friction workflow for deploying a new application quickly, while also supporting long-term scalability. It also offers a marketplace of add-on services, such as databases and monitoring.

There are several similar services to Heroku, some of which we will cover later in this chapter. Heroku was one of the first services of its kind. In particular, it was one of the first to support Node.js as a first-class citizen. It also offers many features for free, including everything needed for the worked example in this section.

 Note that Heroku's free features are sufficient for deploying an application for development, demonstration, or experimental purposes. It would not be sufficient for a production deployment of an application serving end users. See https://www.heroku.com/pricing for details of Heroku's pricing tiers.

# Setting up a Heroku account and tooling

To follow the example in this section, you will first need to sign up for Heroku at https://signup.heroku.com/.

We will also be using the heroku toolbelt, a CLI for configuring Heroku. Download and install the version for your platform from https://toolbelt.heroku.com/.

Check that the heroku toolbelt is installed correctly and available on your path. Open a new command prompt and run the following command:

```
> heroku
```

You should see the help text with a list of available commands. Configure the toolbelt to use your Heroku account by running the following command:

```
> heroku login
```

# Running an application locally with Heroku

Heroku requires a small configuration file (similar to .travis.yml) telling it how to run our application. This is a file named **Procfile**, which in our case contains a single line as follow:

```
web: npm start
```

This tells Heroku that our application consists of a single web process, which can be started with `npm start`.

 Note, especially if you are used to the Windows filesystem, that the uppercase P in the filename is important. The application will be deployed to a Unix-like system, where filenames are case-sensitive.

To verify our `Procfile`, we can run our application locally using Heroku:

```
> heroku local
```

This will launch our application using the `Procfile`. Note that it also sets a default port of `5000`. You should now be able to visit the application at `http://localhost:5000`.

The `heroku local` command also sets up environment variables for our application. These are read from a local `.env` file at the root of our application:

```
MONGODB_URL=mongodb://localhost/hangman
REDIS_URL=redis://127.0.0.1:6379/
```

You can test this by starting up local instances of MongoDB and Redis. Run the following commands in separate prompts (setting the `--dbpath` as appropriate):

```
> redis-server
> mongod --dbpath C:\data\mongodb
> heroku local
```

Having this `.env` file means that we can use `npm start` directly (as we have before) to run with mock datastores and `heroku local` when we want a more realistic environment, without having to keep track of our current environment variables.

# Deploying an application to Heroku

Now that we have created a `Procfile`, deploying our application to the web is easy. First, we need to create a new Heroku application:

```
> heroku create
```

By default, this provisions a minimal application on Heroku, with a randomly assigned name. You can optionally specify an application name as a third parameter.

This command also returns the public URL for our newly-created app, which we can visit now. The following response is returned:

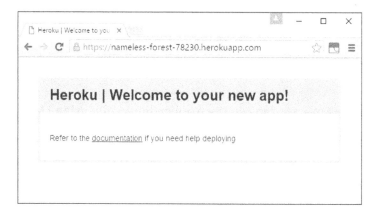

There's not much to see because we haven't deployed anything yet. The quickest way to deploy an application to Heroku is via Git. The `heroku create` command also created a new Git remote for us to push to. You can see this by viewing the list of Git remotes:

```
> git remote -v
```

We now have a Git remote named `heroku`. Make sure the new `Procfile` has been committed. Now, when we push our master branch to this remote, it is automatically built and deployed:

```
> git push heroku master
```

If we visit the application's URL again now, we see the following:

Our application has deployed but is now returning an error. To diagnose the problem with our application, we'll need to look at the logs.

# Working with Heroku logs, config, and services

We can view the logs from our application by running `heroku logs`. If you look through the logs to the error stacktrace, you'll see the following error message:

```
app[web.1]: Error: Cannot find module 'mockgoose'
```

The `mockgoose` package is unavailable because Heroku builds our application using the `dependencies` in `package.json` and not the `devDependencies`. Recall from *Chapter 9*, *Persisting Data*, that this error is intentional. We wanted the application to fail in live environments if no MongoDB URL is configured.

To fix this error, we need to set up a MongoDB instance and configure our application to connect to it. We'll need to do the same for our Redis DB. Both of these data stores are available as services from the Heroku marketplace.

## Setting up MongoDB

We can add Heroku marketplace services via the command line. MongoLab is a third-party service providing MongoDB instances. We can add an instance to our application as follows:

```
> heroku addons:create mongolab:sandbox
```

This creates a sandbox (free tier) MongoDB instance, suitable for demo purposes. Note from the output of this command that it also created a `MONGOLAB_URI` config variable. Heroku will provide this to our application as an environment variable at runtime.

Our application is expecting an environment variable named `MONGODB_URL`. We'll need to create this and set it to the same value as `MONGOLAB_URI`. You can view and set config variables for an application as follows:

```
> heroku config
> heroku config:set MONGODB_URL=mongodb://...
```

You should fill in the value of `MONGODB_URL` to match the value of `MONGOLAB_URI` returned by the first command.

# Setting up Redis

Heroku also provides a Redis service via its marketplace. We'll add it to our application as follows:

```
> heroku addons:create heroku-redis:hobby-dev --as:REDIS
```

Again we use the free tier version of this service (hobby-dev) for demo purposes. It's easy to re-scale services to different tiers later.

The Redis service also allows you to specify an alias for the created service instance. Aliases are specified using the `--as` parameter with `heroku addons:create`. This is useful for Redis as we may have several Redis instances associated with a single application. It's particularly useful for us, since, by aliasing our instance as REDIS, Heroku will create a `REDIS_URL` environment variable. This is exactly what our application expects to see.

The `heroku addons:create` command restarts our application immediately. Our new database instances will take a minute or two to become available though. Wait a minute before restarting the application:

```
> heroku restart
```

We can now visit the application URL in our browser and see it running on the Web!

# Deploying from Travis CI

Deploying via Git is a quick way to get up and running and is useful for developers. It's not a robust way of pushing out changes though. If we are practicing Continuous Delivery then we may want to deploy on every commit, at least to a UAT environment. But we still want our CI server to act as a gatekeeper and ensure that we only deploy good builds.

Travis CI supports deployment to a wide range of hosting providers (as well as arbitrary deployment via custom scripts). We can tell Travis CI to deploy to Heroku by adding a `deploy` section to our `travis.yml` as follows (replacing `application-name-12345` with the name of our previously created Heroku application):

```
services:
- mongodb
- redis-server
deploy:
  provider: heroku
  app: application-name-12345
  api_key:
env:
  global:
  - MONGODB_URL=mongodb://localhost/hangman
  - REDIS_URL=redis://127.0.0.1:6379/
```

Travis CI will only deploy our application if the build passes. In order for Travis CI to communicate with Heroku, it requires our Heroku API key. But we may not want to commit this to source control (especially if our Git repository is public). Travis CI allows you to avoid this by specifying encrypted environment variables for the build.

# Setting encrypted Travis CI environment variables

Environment variables can be encrypted using a public key that Travis CI associates with our repository. Travis CI then uses the corresponding private key to decrypt these variables at build time.

The easiest way to encrypt environment variables with the correct key is to use the Travis CLI. This is available as a Ruby package.

# Installing Ruby

If you do not have Ruby installed on your system already, see
`https://www.ruby-lang.org/en/documentation/installation/`. The best way
to install on Windows is to use `RubyInstaller`, from `http://rubyinstaller.org/`.

You can check whether Ruby is installed and configured on your path by running
the following command:

```
> ruby -ver
```

You should have version 2.0.0 or higher.

# Creating an encrypted environment variable

Once you have Ruby installed and on your path, you can install the Travis CLI
as follows:

```
> gem install travis --no-rdoc --no-ri
```

>  **Gem** is the Ruby package manager, similar to npm. The `--no-doc`
> and `--no-ri` arguments here skip installation of low-level API
> docs, which we don't need.

Now we can add our encrypted environment variable. First we need to obtain the
Heroku API key for our application:

```
> heroku auth:token
```

Now we can add this to our `.travis.yml` file as follows:

```
> travis encrypt [AUTH_TOKEN] --add deploy.api_key
```

`[AUTH_TOKEN]` is the output from the previous command.

This encrypts the API key and automatically adds the encrypted version into our
`.travis.yml` file. Before committing, try updating something in the application, for
example the page title from `src/routes/index.js`:

```
    . . .
            .then(results => {
                res.render('index', {
                        title: 'Hangman online',
                        userId: req.user.id,
                        createdGames: results[0],
    . . .
```

Now commit and push the master branch (to `origin`, not directly to `heroku`) and wait for the Travis CI build to complete. The build output shows our application being deployed:

```
1010  [12:12:38] Finished 'test' after 1.76 s
1011  [12:12:38] Starting 'default'...
1012  [12:12:38] Finished 'default' after 9.2 µs
1013  [12:12:38] Starting 'integration-test'...
1014  [12:12:39] Finished 'integration-test' after 1.19 s
1015
1016
1017  The command "gulp default integration-test" exited with 0.
1018  Fetching: dpl-1.8.11.gem (100%)                          dpl.0
1022                                                           24.89s
1023  Installing deploy dependencies                           dpl.1
1035  Preparing deploy                                         dpl.2
1042  Deploying application                                    dpl.3
1110  Already up-to-date!
1111  # HEAD detached at 475853f
1112  nothing to commit, working directory clean
1113  Dropped refs/stash@{0} (53cc1305f2a045bc92e306e1b8741c08e4304060)
1114
1115
1116  Done. Your build exited with 0.
                                                              Top ▲
```

If you visit the application again, you should see the new version with the updated title.

Recall that Travis CI is actually building our application for multiple versions of Node.js. By default, Travis CI deploys our application at the end of each build job. This is unnecessary and slows down our overall build. We can tell Travis CI to deploy only from a specific build job by altering our `.travis.yml` file as follows:

```
deploy:
  provider: heroku
  app: afternoon-cliffs-85674
  on:
    node: 6
  api_key:
    secure: ...
```

If we commit and check the output from Travis CI again, we can see that only the Node.js v6 build job performs a deployment.

# Further resources

For further considerations on deploying web apps, see The Twelve-Factor App (`http://12factor.net/`). This is a detailed resource about important considerations for running enterprise-grade web applications on services such as Heroku.

There are, of course, a great many options for hosting a web application. Azure's web app service and AWS's Elastic Beanstalk both support Node.js as a first-class citizen. Modulus (`https://modulus.io/`) provides Node.js and Mongo DB hosting, with powerful scaling, monitoring, and load-balancing features.

The preceding are all examples of application hosting platforms (**Platform-as-a-Service (PaaS)**, in cloud terminology). You can, of course, also deploy Node.js applications to bare infrastructure (either cloud infrastructure or your own machines). For a detailed guide, see `https://certsimple.com/blog/deploy-node-on-linux`.

You may need to manage releases of your application through multiple environments. Your CI server might first deploy your application to an integration environment and run tests on it there before deploying to UAT. You may then want to be able to push the exact same release from UAT to Stage and Live environments at the click of a button.

Heroku Pipelines and Azure Web App deployment slots allow you to manage the release of your application through different environments. **Wercker** (`http://wercker.com/`) is a build and deployment service that can automate more complex workflows. It also provides isolated environments based on Docker containers.

# Summary

In this chapter, we have deployed an application to the web using Heroku, configured environment settings and provisioned databases, set up Travis CI to automatically deploy successful builds, and learned about further options and considerations for deploying Node.js applications.

Now that our application is available online, we can start thinking about how to integrate it with the wider Web. In the next chapter, we'll look at allowing users to log in using third party social media services as an identity provider.

# 12
# Authentication in Node.js

The application we have built so far allows users to choose a username to identify themselves. However, they only retain this identity for the duration of their browser session. It's important to allow users to retain a consistent identity from one session to the next. This allows us to build richer user experiences. Some websites (such as Facebook) couldn't offer their main functionality at all without being able to identify users.

Identifying users requires us to implement authentication. In this chapter, we will cover the following topics:

- Implementing third-party authentication via social networking sites
- Associating third-party identities with our own user data
- Simulating user authentication to support integration testing

## Introducing Passport

Passport is an authentication framework for Node.js. It can act as Express middleware, making it easy to integrate with our application.

Like some of the other libraries we've discussed so far, Passport is very modular. Its core package provides a common paradigm for authentication. Passport's middleware performs authentication and augments the request object with a `user` property.

Additional Passport npm packages support hundreds of different **strategies** for authentication. Each Passport strategy provides a different mechanism for identifying users. We'll look at a few of these strategies in this chapter. Passport makes it easy to add new strategies to suit the needs of each application.

# Choosing an authentication strategy

A common introductory example is username/password-based authentication. This uses a login form to verify users' credentials against the application's database. Although this is one of the simplest authentication mechanisms to understand, it's not the most useful. Forcing users to create an account for our site is an extra hurdle to them using it. Users also get tired of creating an account and picking a password for every new website.

Passport does support this kind of authentication, via the `passport-local` strategy. We'll make use of this strategy for test purposes later on in this chapter, but not in our production code. It's better to allow users to authenticate using an identity already established elsewhere. This saves users from having to pick new credentials and also saves our website from having to manage these. This is just good separation of concerns.

If you log in to StackOverflow, you'll notice that it suggests logging in using Google+ or Facebook. It also supports OpenID and other providers. Implementing support for each of these login mechanisms from scratch would be a lot of work. Fortunately there are Passport strategies for all of them.

# Understanding third-party authentication

Passport will do most of the heavy lifting for us, but it's still worth having a basic understanding of how third-party authentication works. When a client wants to log into a website, it sends them to a third-party provider. The third-party provider gives the client back a token they can use to authenticate with the website. When the client is a web browser, this process can be made almost invisible to the user, via automatic redirects.

The website must then verify that the token presented to it by the client really came from the third-party provider. The website and the third-party provider might have established a pre-shared key for this purpose, which could be used to create a cryptographically verifiable token. Alternatively, the website might call the third-party provider directly to verify the token. In practice, a website will often want to call a third-party provider anyway to gain more information associated with the user's identity, for example, their username or other profile information.

# Using Express sessions

Many of Passport's strategies are based on HTTP sessions. At the moment, our application is just using simple cookies to store user IDs. To use Passport for third-party authentication, we'll need to add session support into our application. Express provides session support in the `express-session` module. First, we add this to our application:

```
> npm install express-session --save
```

We also need somewhere to store session data. Express supports a variety of session stores via additional modules. Redis is well suited to this task and we already have a Redis instance available. We can use the `connect-redis` module to store sessions in Redis:

```
> npm install connect-redis --save
```

We can now create a new configuration module to keep all our session logic in one place. Since this will return middleware, we'll put it in the `middleware` folder here `src/middleware/sessions.js`:

```
'use strict';

const session = require('express-session');

let config = {
    secret: process.env.SESSION_SECRET,
    saveUninitialized: false,
    resave: false
};

if (process.env.REDIS_URL && process.env.NODE_ENV !== 'test') {
    const RedisStore = require('connect-redis')(session);
    config.store = new RedisStore({ url: process.env.REDIS_URL });
}

module.exports = session(config);
```

We configure the Express `session` module as follows:

* Use the value of an environment variable as the session secret
* Only save sessions that contain some data
* Do not resave sessions unless they have changed
* If Redis is available, use it as the session store

Let's consider each of the configuration properties in turn.

# Specifying a session secret

Express uses a session secret to protect session data from being tampering with. You should specify this by setting the SESSION_SECRET environment variable locally. The value is arbitrary and can be anything, as long as it's not empty. We also need to specify this in our integration test so it can run on the CI server. The following code is from gulpfile.js:

```
gulp.task('integration-test', ..., (done) => {
    const TEST_PORT = 5000;
    process.env.SESSION_SECRET =
        process.env.SESSION_SECRET || 'testOnly';
    require('./src/server.js').then((server) => {
        ...
    });
});
```

# Deciding when the session gets saved

Avoiding unnecessary saves is a minor optimization and can avoid certain race conditions. Only saving initialized sessions allows you to request user consent before storing any cookies. This might be necessary for compliance with regional laws, most notably in the EU. See https://www.cookiechoices.org/ for more information.

# Using alternative session stores

By default, Express will use an in-memory session store. This is fine for development purposes and in test environments where we only have one application process, but is not suitable for production use. Storing sessions out of process in Redis is important if we want to scale across multiple instances. We configure the Redis store with our existing Redis URL.

In practice, you might want to use different Redis instances for session data and other application data. These are quite different use cases, so they might benefit from a different configuration of Redis. For example, session data is likely to be higher load, but can afford to be more volatile. For small-scale applications such as our example application in this book, a single Redis instance will suffice.

# Using session middleware

We can now use sessions elsewhere in our application instead of directly setting cookies. The following code is from `src/app.js`:

```
let sessions = require('./middleware/sessions');
...
app.use(bodyParser.urlencoded({ extended: false }));
app.use(sessions);
app.use(express.static(path.join(__dirname, 'public')));
...
```

The following code is from `src/middleware/users.js`:

```
'use strict';

module.exports = (service) => {
    const uuid = require('uuid');

    return function(req, res, next) {
        let userId = req.session.userId;
        if (!userId) {
            userId = uuid.v4();
            req.session.userId = userId;
            req.user = {
                id: userId
            };
            next();
        } else {
            ...
        }
    };
};
```

The following code is from `src/server.js`:

```
'use strict';

module.exports = require('./config/mongoose').then(mongoose => {
    ...
    io.use(adapt(require('./middleware/sessions')));
    const usersService = require('./services/users.js');
    ...
});
```

# Implementing social login

For our first example, we'll use Twitter as our third-party authentication provider. If you want to follow along with the example you will need a Twitter account, which is very quick to set up.

## Setting up a Twitter application

In order for Twitter to recognize our application, we need to create a new app in Twitter's developer portal:

1. Visit `https://apps.twitter.com/` and click on **Create New App**.

2. Fill in the Name, Description, Website, and Callback URL fields:

   ° If you've deployed your application to Heroku, you can use its Heroku URL here

   ° Otherwise, just fill in placeholder values for both fields (for example, `http://test.example.com/callback`)

3. Click on **Create your Twitter application**.

4. Click on the **Settings** tab and ensure that **Enable Callback Locking** is unchecked (leaving this unchecked allows you to use placeholder values for the URLs and is also useful for local testing).

5. Click on the **Keys and Access Tokens** tab to view your application's **Consumer Key (API Key)** and **Consumer Secret (API Secret)**.

Set new local environment variables named `TWITTER_API_KEY` and `TWITTER_API_SECRET`, containing the corresponding values from Twitter. You might want to create a shell script or batch file to set these in the console or configure them as Heroku environment variables (see *Chapter 11*, *Deploying Node.js Applications*)

## Configuring Passport

We'll now make use of Passport to allow users to log into our site via Twitter. First, we need to install the relevant npm packages:

```
> npm install passport --save
> npm install passport-twitter --save
```

Now we can configure Passport to authenticate with Twitter. We add the following code under `src/config/passport.js`:

```
'use strict';

const passport = require('passport');
const TwitterStrategy = require('passport-twitter').Strategy;

module.exports = (usersService) => {
    if (process.env.TWITTER_API_KEY &&
            process.env.TWITTER_API_SECRET) {
        passport.use(new TwitterStrategy({
            consumerKey: process.env.TWITTER_API_KEY,
            consumerSecret: process.env.TWITTER_API_SECRET,
            callbackURL: '/auth/twitter/callback',
            passReqToCallback: true
        }, (req, token, tokenSecret, profile, done) => {
            usersService.setUsername(req.user.id,
                    profile.username || profile.displayName)
                .then(() => { done(); }, done);
        }));
    }
    return passport;
};
```

This uses the `TwitterStrategy` for authentication with Twitter, passing in our API key and secret on a configuration object. The second constructor parameter is a function that Passport will invoke after authenticating with Twitter (referred to as the **verify callback** in Passport's documentation). Here we set the current user's name based on the `profile.username` or `profile.displayName` provided from Twitter by Passport.

 The `profile` object contains the user profile returned by the authentication provider. Passport standardizes profile data to make it easier to work with multiple strategies. There's a standard set of fields, such as `displayName`, which all Passport strategies will populate if possible. We'd prefer to use the Twitter username (for example, hgcummings) than the display name (for example, Harry Cummings). The `profile.username` field contains the Twitter username. This is not one of the standard fields, but many strategies will return a field with this name. So we use `profile.username` first, but fall back to the more standard `profile.displayName`.

Now we just need to make use of our new passport module in Express. The following code is from `src/app.js`:

```
let passport = require('./config/passport')(usersService);
...

app.use(users);
app.use(passport.initialize());
app.post('/auth/twitter', passport.authenticate('twitter'));
app.get('/auth/twitter/callback',
    passport.authenticate('twitter',
        { successRedirect: '/', failureRedirect: '/' }));

app.use('/', routes);
...
```

This tells our application to do three things:

- Use Passport's Express middleware
- Authenticate users via Twitter when they POST to `/auth/twitter`
- Handle Twitter authentication results at `/auth/twitter/callback` before redirecting users to the homepage

Finally, we need to provide a login button to reach our new endpoint as shown here in `src/views/index.js`:

```
<h1>{{ title }}</h1>
<h2>Account</h2>
{{#ranking}}
    ...
{{/ranking}}
<form action="/auth/twitter" method="POST">
    <input type="submit" value="Log in using Twitter" />
</form>
<h3>Profile</h3>
<form action="/profile" method="POST">
    ...
</form>
...
```

If you run the application and click **Log in using Twitter**, the following will happen:

- The application will redirect your browser to Twitter
- Twitter will prompt you to log in if you have not already
- Twitter will ask whether you're happy with the application seeing your profile details and other public data
- Twitter will then redirect your browser to the `/auth/twitter/callback` endpoint
- Your browser will make a request to this endpoint with your authentication token from Twitter
- Passport will validate this token then invoke our login handler function
- When our function completes, Passport will return a redirect response to the homepage

We have now integrated Twitter authentication with our application! However, we're not really using it to allow users to log in. We're just associating a Twitter username with our existing user IDs created for each session. You can see this by opening up two separate browser sessions. Try logging in with each of them. If you create a new game in one browser, it appears in the other browser in the list of games created by other users. This is because you now have two user IDs associated with the same Twitter username.

We need to recognize the same user whenever they log in with the same Twitter account. This should not depend on being in the same browser session. To address this, we'll need to do the following:

- Persist user accounts to our database
- Tell Passport how to store and retrieve users
- Let Passport associate a user with the current session

# Persisting user data with Redis

We already use Redis to associate usernames with user IDs. Now we want to be able to associate user IDs with Twitter accounts as well. The first time a user logs in with an external provider, we want to create a new user with the name taken from the external profile. Subsequent requests authenticated with the same provider will see the same user.

We can implement this functionality using Redis's SETNX operation. This will only set a key if it does not already exist and return whether this was the case. Our implementation is as follows from src/services/users.js:

```
'use strict';

const redisClient = require('../config/redis.js');
const uuid = require('uuid');

const getUser = userId =>
  redisClient.getAsync(`user:${userId}:name`)
    .then(userName => ({
      id: userId,
      name: userName
    }));

const setUsername = (userId, name) =>
  redisClient.setAsync(`user:${userId}:name`, name);

module.exports = {
  getOrCreate: (provider, providerId, providerUsername) => {
    let providerKey = `provider:${provider}:${providerId}:user`;
    let newUserId = uuid.v4();
    return redisClient.setnxAsync(providerKey, newUserId)
      .then(created => {
        if (created) {
          return setUsername(newUserId, providerUsername)
            .then(() => getUser(newUserId));
        } else {
          return redisClient
            .getAsync(providerKey).then(getUser);
        }
      });
  },
  getUser: getUser,    getUsername: userId => redisClient.getAsync(`us
er:${userId}:name`),
  setUsername: setUsername,
  ...
};
```

Here, we create a new user ID and tell Redis to associate it with the external provider (for example, Twitter) account. If we have seen the external account before, we return the user that was already associated with it. Otherwise, we persist a new user ID and associate it with the username from the external profile. Tests for this functionality can be found in the companion code.

# Configuring Passport with persistence

Now that we have a way of persisting users, we need to tell Passport how to make use of this. First, we update our verify callback to make use of our new `getOrCreate` function rather than just setting a username. Then we need to tell Passport how to identify and retrieve users associated with a session by serializing users to and from a string. The following code is from `src/config/passport.js`:

```
'use strict';

const passport = require('passport');
const TwitterStrategy = require('passport-twitter').Strategy;

module.exports = (usersService) => {
    if(process.env.TWITTER_API_KEY &&
            process.env.TWITTER_API_SECRET) {
        passport.use(new TwitterStrategy({
            consumerKey: process.env.TWITTER_API_KEY,
            consumerSecret: process.env.TWITTER_API_SECRET,
            callbackURL: '/auth/twitter/callback',
            passReqToCallback: true
        }, (req, token, tokenSecret, profile, done) => {
            usersService.getOrCreate('twitter', profile.id,
                    profile.username || profile.displayName)
                .then(user => done(null, user), done);
        }));
    }

    passport.serializeUser((user, done) => {
        done(null, user.id);
    });

    passport.deserializeUser((id, done) => {
        usersService.getUser(id)
            .then(user => done(null, user))
            .catch(done);
    });

    return passport;
};
```

Passport stores the string version of the user (returned by our `serializeUser` callback) on the session. It uses our `deserializeUser` callback to turn this string into a user object which it adds to the request. In our case, the string representation of the user is just their ID and deserialization is just a lookup in the users service.

In order for this to work, we also need to tell our application to use Passport's own session middleware, which works together with Express sessions. To avoid repetition, we'll specify all of our session-related middleware in our session middleware module. The following is the code from `src/middleware/sessions.js`:

```
...

const expressSession = session(config);
module.exports = passport => [
    expressSession, passport.initialize(), passport.session()
];
```

This module now returns three middleware instances. We want to use this with both Express and Socket.IO. The first of these is simple, since we can pass multiple middleware objects to the Express `app.use` function as here `src/app.js`:

```
...
let passport = require('./config/passport')(usersService);
let sessions = require('./middleware/sessions')(passport);
...
app.use(bodyParser.json());
app.use(bodyParser.urlencoded({ extended: false }));
app.use(sessions);
app.use(express.static(path.join(__dirname, 'public')));

app.post('/auth/twitter', passport.authenticate('twitter'));
...
```

For Socket.IO, we need to adapt each middleware in turn as here `src/server.js`:

```
...
const usersService = require('./services/users.js');
let passport = require('./config/passport');
require('./middleware/sessions')(passport).forEach(
    middleware => io.use(adapt(middleware)));

require('./realtime/chat')(io);
...
```

Note that, in both cases, our users middleware is no longer needed and can now be deleted. However, this middleware previously ensured that there was always a user object on the request. This will now only be the case when there is a logged in user, so we need to update the rest of our application accordingly.

There are a few places in our application that assume there will always be a user on the request. Since this is no longer guaranteed, there are two ways to resolve this: we can update our code to cope with no user being present on the request or we can hide functionality from unauthenticated users.

We still want unauthenticated users to be able to view public chat and to see and play games, so we update this functionality accordingly. The code from `src/realtime/chat.js` is updated as follows:

```
namespace.on('connection', (socket) => {
    let username = null;
    if (socket.request.user) {
        username = socket.request.user.name;
    }
    ...
```

The following code is from `src/realtime/games.js`:

```
function forwardEvent(name, socket) {
    service.events.on(name, game => {
        if (!socket.request.user ||
                game.setBy !== socket.request.user.id) {
            socket.emit(name, game.id);
        }
    });
}
```

The following code is from `src/routes/games.js`:

```
router.post('/:id/guesses', function(req, res, next) {
    checkGameExists(
        req.params.id,
        res,
        game => {
            if (req.user && game.matches(req.body.word)) {
                userService.recordWin(req.user.id);
            }
            ...
        },
        next
    );
});
```

# Hiding functionality from unauthenticated users

We certainly want unauthenticated users to be able to visit the home page of our application, but might not want to display all of the application's functionality to them. To achieve this, we'll update our index route as follows from `src/routes/index.js`:

```
router.get('/', function(req, res, next) {
    let userId = null;
    if (req.user) {
        userId = req.user.id;
    }

    Promise.all([gamesService.createdBy(userId),
                gamesService.availableTo(userId),
                usersService.getUsername(userId),
                usersService.getRanking(userId),
                usersService.getTopPlayers()])
        .then(results => {
            res.render('index', {
                    title: 'Hangman online',
                    loggedIn: req.isAuthenticated(),
                    createdGames: results[0],
                    ...
                });
        })
        .catch(next);
});
```

Note that this adds a `loggedIn` property to the view data instead of the user ID. The value of this property comes from the `isAuthenticated` function, which is added to the request by Passport. We use this to hide features that will no longer work for unauthenticated users and hide the login button from authenticated users. The following code is from `src/views/index.hjs`:

```
    ...
    <body>
        ...
    {{^loggedIn}}
      <form action="/auth/twitter" method="POST">
        <input type="submit" value="Log in using Twitter" />
      </form>
    {{/loggedIn}}
```

```
{{#loggedIn}}
  <h3>Profile</h3>
  <form action="/profile" method="POST">
    ...
  </form>
{{/loggedIn}}
<h2>Games</h2>
{{#loggedIn}}
  <form action="/games" method="POST" id="createGame">
    ...
  </form>
  <h3>Games created by you</h3>
  ...
{{/loggedIn}}
<h3>Games available to play</h3>
...
<h2>Top players</h2>
...
<h3>Lobby</h3>
<form class="chat" data-room="lobby">
  <div id="messages"></dl>
  {{#loggedIn}}
    <input id="message"/><input type="submit" value="Send"/>
  {{/loggedIn}}
</form>
</body>
</html>
```

# Integration testing with Passport

We still have one problem, which is that our integration tests won't work anymore. Only logged-in users can create games now. It would be a good idea to write a new integration test to check that Twitter authentication works. We don't want to introduce a Twitter account dependency to our current test though.

Instead, we'll make use of the passport-local strategy to allow our test to log in. We'll install this as a dev dependency so it can't accidentally run in production:

```
> npm install passport-local --save-dev
```

We configure Passport to accept any username and password. If using passport-local for real, this is where you would check against credentials in your data store. The following code is from `src/config/passport.js`:

```
if (process.env.NODE_ENV === 'test') {
   const LocalStrategy = require('passport-local');
   const uuid = require('uuid');
   passport.use(new LocalStrategy((username, password, done) => {
         const userId = uuid.v4();
         usersService.setUsername(userId, username)
            .then(() => {
                done(null, { id: userId, name: username });
            });
      }
   ));
}
```

Then we add a new local authentication endpoint to our application as here `src/app.js`:

```
if (process.env.NODE_ENV === 'test') {
  app.post('/auth/test',
    passport.authenticate('local', { successRedirect: '/' }));
}
```

And finally update our test to login as a first step as code from `integration-test/game.js` shown follows:

```
function withGame(word, callback) {
    page.open(rootUrl + '/auth/test',
        'POST',
        'username=TestUser&password=dummy',
        function() {
            ...
        }
    );
}
```

# Allowing users to log out

Users will also expect us to provide a way to log out of our application. Passport makes this easy by adding a `logout` function to the request. We just need to make use of this in one of our routes here `src/routes/index.js`:

```
router.post('/logout', function(req, res){
    req.logout();
```

```
                res.redirect('/');
        });
```

We can add a log out button to our view to make use of this new route as in `src/views/index.hjs`:

```
{{#loggedIn}}
  <form action="/logout" method="POST">
    <input type="submit" value="Log out" />
  </form>
  <h3>Profile</h3>
```

# Adding other login providers

Now that we have all the general infrastructure for authentication, adding additional providers is easy. Let's add Facebook authentication as an example. First, we need to install the relevant Passport strategy:

```
> npm install passport-facebook --save
```

Then we can update our Passport config file from `src/config/passport.js` as follows:

```
...
const FacebookStrategy = require('passport-facebook').Strategy;

module.exports = (usersService) => {
    const providerCallback = providerName =>
        function(req, token, tokenSecret, profile, done) {
            usersService.getOrCreate(providerName, profile.id,
                    profile.username || profile.displayName)
                .then(user => done(null, user), done);
        };

    if(process.env.TWITTER_API_KEY &&
            process.env.TWITTER_API_SECRET) {
        passport.use(new TwitterStrategy({
            consumerKey: process.env.TWITTER_API_KEY,
            consumerSecret: process.env.TWITTER_API_SECRET,
            callbackURL: '/auth/twitter/callback',
            passReqToCallback: true
        }, providerCallback('twitter')));
    }
```

```
if(process.env.FACEBOOK_APP_ID &&
        process.env.FACEBOOK_APP_SECRET) {
    passport.use(new FacebookStrategy({
        clientID: process.env.FACEBOOK_APP_ID,
        clientSecret: process.env.FACEBOOK_APP_SECRET,
        callbackURL: '/auth/facebook/callback',
        passReqToCallback: true
    }, providerCallback('facebook')));
}
...
};
```

Here we've generalized our verify callback function to take different provider names, then used this with both Twitter and Facebook authentication strategies. We can re-use this to add further strategies in the same way. We just need to set the relevant environment variables for them to work.

To obtain a Facebook App ID and Secret, create a new Facebook application at https://developers.facebook.com/apps/ (which requires you to have a Facebook account). This is very similar to the process for Twitter. Just create a new application of type Website, with a URL that matches your development environment (for example, http://localhost:3000). Once created, the App ID and App Secret will be visible on the Dashboard page for the application.

We also need to add Facebook authentication routes to our application config file. These are just the same as the corresponding Twitter routes. As with the Passport config file, we can commonize by parameterizing the provider name. The code from src/app.js is as follows:

```
app.use(sessions);
const addAuthEndpoints = provider => {
    app.post(`/auth/${provider}`, passport.authenticate(provider));
    app.get(`/auth/${provider}/callback`,
        passport.authenticate(provider, { successRedirect: '/',
            failureRedirect: '/', session: true }));
};
addAuthEndpoints('twitter');
addAuthEndpoints('facebook');
```

Finally, we need to add a button to allow users to log in with Facebook. The following code is from `src/views/index.hjs`:

```
{{^loggedIn}}
  <form action="/auth/twitter" method="POST">
    <input type="submit" value="Log in using Twitter" />
  </form>
  <form action="/auth/facebook" method="POST">
    <input type="submit" value="Log in using Facebook" />
  </form>
{{/loggedIn}}
```

Adding additional providers is easy. To add Google+ authentication, we would just need to follow these steps:

1. Install the `passport-google` npm module

2. Create a new application as described at `https://developers.google.com/identity/protocols/OpenIDConnect`

3. Update the three files listed above, passing the Google provider to our new common functions

# Summary

In this chapter, we have added authentication to our Express application using Passport, introduced Express sessions using Redis for session storage, leveraged multiple Passport strategies to support different external providers, and persisted user data in Redis.

This completes our example web application. In the next chapter we will look at how to create different kinds of Node.js project: a library and a command-line tool.

# 13
# Creating JavaScript Packages

So far we have built up a web application, making use of various npm packages along the way. These packages include libraries such as Express and command-line tools such as Gulp. Now we'll look at how to go about creating packages of our own.

In this chapter we will:

- Explore the different module systems available for JavaScript
- Create our own JavaScript library
- Write JavaScript that can run on both the client and server-side
- Create a command-line tool in JavaScript
- Release a new npm package
- Use Node.js modules in the browser environment

 The code examples in this chapter are independent of everything we've done so far.

## Writing universal modules

We have already written many of our own modules as part of our application. We can also write library modules for use in other applications.

When writing code for use by others, it's worth considering in what contexts it will be useful. Some libraries are only useful in specific environments. For example, Express is server-specific and jQuery is browser-specific. But many modules provide functionality that would be useful in any environment, for example, utility modules such as the `uuid` module we've used elsewhere in this book.

Let's look at writing a module to work in multiple environments. We'll need to support more than just Node.js-style modules. We'll also need to support client-side module systems such as RequireJS. Recall from *Chapter 4*, *Introducing Node.js Modules*, that Node.js and RequireJS implement two different module standards (CommonJS and **Asynchronous Module Definition** (**AMD**), respectively). Our package may also be used client-side in a website with no module system in place.

As an example, let's create a module providing a simple `flatMap` method. This will work like `SelectMany` in .NET's LINQ. It will take an array and a function that returns a new array for each element. It will return a single array of the combined results.

As a Node.js/CommonJS module, we could implement this as follows:

```
module.exports = function flatMap(source, callback) {
    return Array.prototype.concat.apply([], source.map(callback));
}
```

# Comparing Node.js and RequireJS

Recall from *Chapter 4*, *Introducing Node.js Modules*, that each module system provides the following:

- A way of declaring a module with a name and its own scope
- A way of defining functionality provided by the module
- A way of importing a module into another script

Node.js implements the CommonJS module standard. Module names correspond to file paths and each file has its own scope. Modules define the functionality they provide using the `exports` alias. Modules are imported using the `require` function.

RequireJS is designed for the browser environment. In the browser there is no new scope per file (all script files execute in the same scope and can see the same variables). Also, modules must be loaded by network requests rather than from the local filesystem.

RequireJS implements the AMD standard. AMD specifies two functions, which RequireJS adds to the top-level window object in the browser environment:

- The `define` function allows new modules to be created by providing a name and a factory function for the module. The scope of the module will be the scope of its factory function. The functionality of the module is defined by the return value of the factory function.

- The `require` function allows modules to be imported. Although this has the same name as the module import function in Node.js, it works very differently. Multiple module names can be specified for import (as an array). The require function is asynchronous and takes a callback to be executed when all the dependencies are loaded. This allows RequireJS to load modules efficiently in the browser environment.

# Supporting the browser environment

For our module to work in the browser environment, we need to support the AMD standard so RequireJS can work. We also need to accommodate sites not using any module loader. We can achieve this by extending our module definition as follows, in `scripts/flatMap.js`:

```
(function (root, factory) {
    'use strict';
    if (typeof define === 'function' && define.amd) {
        define([], factory);
    } else if (typeof module === 'object' && module.exports) {
        module.exports = factory();
    } else {
        root.flatMap = factory();
    }
}(this, function () {
    'use strict';
    return function flatMap(source, clbk) {
        return Array.prototype.concat.apply([], source.map(clbk));
    }
}));
```

 Note the use of an anonymous function that is invoked straight away, called an **Immediately-Invoked Function Expression (IIFE)**. This is a common way of creating an isolated scope in JavaScript environments without built-in modules.

First, we check for the existence of an AMD-style `define` function (the existence of a `define.amd` property is also specified by the AMD standard). Note that the asynchronous nature of the `define` function means that we need to use a factory function to create our module. We provide a list of dependencies (empty in this case) and our factory function to the `define` function to create our module.

If no AMD module system is present, we check for the CommonJS-style `module.exports` used by Node.js. Finally, if neither module system is present, we provide our module as a property on the `root` parameter. Our argument for this parameter is the `this` keyword evaluated in the global scope. In a browser, this will be the `window` object.

# Using AMD modules with RequireJS

Let's create a simple web page to check that our module works correctly with RequireJS. We'll also show how to use RequireJS with an external library, jQuery.

First we define an HTML file for the page:

```
<!DOCTYPE html>
<html>
    <head>
        <script data-main="scripts/main" src="https://cdnjs.
cloudflare.com/ajax/libs/require.js/2.1.22/require.min.js"></script>
        <style>input, pre { display: block; margin: 0.5em auto; width:
320px; }</style>
    </head>
    <body>
        <input type="text" />
        <input type="text" />
        <input type="text" />
        <input type="text" />
        <pre id="wordcounts"></pre>
    </body>
</html>
```

Note that the only script tag on the page is for RequireJS itself. This script tag also has a data attribute indicating the entry point of our application. The path `scripts/main` tells RequireJS to load `scripts/main.js`, which contains the following:

```
requirejs.config({
    paths: {
        jquery: 'https://cdnjs.cloudflare.com/ajax/libs/jquery/2.2.1/
jquery.min'
    }
```

```
});

require(['flatMap', 'jquery'], function(flatMap, $) {
    $('input').change(function() {
        var allText = $.map($('input'), function(input) {
            return $(input).val();
        }).filter(function(text) {
            return !!text;
        });
        var allWords = flatMap(allText, function(text) {
            return text.split(' ');
        });
        var counts = {};
        allWords.forEach(function(word) {
            counts[word] = (counts[word] || 0) + 1;
        });
        $('#wordcounts').text(JSON.stringify(counts));
    })
});
```

This script first configures RequireJS. The only `config` property specified here is the `path` property. The path for jQuery under the key `'jquery'` tells RequireJS how to resolve the `'jquery'` dependency. We don't need to specify a path for `flatMap.js` because we have saved it under the same directory as `main.js`.

Next we use the `require` function to load flatMap and jQuery and pass them into our main application function. In larger applications using RequireJS, this is usually a very short bootstrap function. The `main.js` file is also often the only place that you'll see a `require` call. Most of the application code is in modules declared with `define`.

As this is just a test of our library with RequireJS, we'll put the rest of our application code inside our main application function. We use our flatMap module and jQuery to calculate and display word counts across all the text inputs. You can see this working by opening `index.html` in your browser:

| |
|---|
| red lorry |
| yellow lorry |
| red lorry |
| yellow lolly |
| {"red":2,"lorry":3,"yellow":2,"lolly":1} |

# Isomorphic JavaScript

The `flatMap.js` example above is an implementation of the Universal Module Definition pattern. See `https://github.com/umdjs/umd` for annotated templates for this pattern. These templates also show how to declare dependencies between modules that follow this pattern.

More generally, writing code that achieves the same result both on the server and in the browser is referred to as **Isomorphic JavaScript**. See `http://isomorphic.net/` for more explanation and examples of this principle.

# Writing npm packages

If you create some code that would be useful to others, you can distribute it as an npm package. To demonstrate this, we'll implement some slightly more complex functionality.

> You can find the example code for this section at `https://github.com/NodeJsForDevelopers/autotoc`. Note that, unlike previous chapters, there is not one per commit per heading. The listings in the rest of this section match the final version of the code.

We're going to implement a tool for generating a **table of contents (ToC)** by crawling a website. To help with this, we'll make use of a few other npm packages:

- **request** provides an API for making HTTP requests, which is higher-level and much simpler to use than the build in the Node.js http module

- **cheerio** provides jQuery-like HTML traversal outside of the browser environment

- **denodeify**, mentioned in *Chapter 8, Mastering Asynchronicity*, allows us to use the request library with promises instead of callbacks

> It's common for npm packages to depend on other packages in this way. But it is worth minimizing your package's dependencies if you want it to be appealing to other developers. Packages with many transitive dependencies can add a lot of bloat to applications, and make it harder for developers to be confident that they understand everything they are pulling into their application.

The code for our module follows, as given in `autotoc.js`:

```
'use strict';

const cheerio = require('cheerio');
const request = require('denodeify')(require('request'));
const url = require('url');

class Page {
  constructor(name, url) {
    this.name = name;
    this.url = url;
    this.children = [];
  }

  spider() {
    return request(this.url)
      .then(response => {
        let $ = cheerio.load(response.body);
        let promiseChildren = [];
        $('a').each((i, elem) => {
          let name = $(elem).contents().get(0).nodeValue;
          let childUrl = $(elem).attr('href');
          if (name && childUrl && childUrl !== '/') {
            let absoluteUrl = url.resolve(this.url, childUrl);
            if (absoluteUrl.indexOf(this.url) === 0 &&
                absoluteUrl !== this.url) {
              let childPage = new Page(name.trim(), absoluteUrl);
              if (childUrl.indexOf('#') === 0) {
                promiseChildren.push(Promise.resolve(childPage));
              } else {
                promiseChildren.push(childPage.spider());
              }
            }
          }
        });
        return Promise.all(promiseChildren).then(children => {
          this.children = children;
          return this;
        });
      });
  }
}

module.exports = baseUrl => new Page('Home', baseUrl).spider();
```

It's not important to understand every single line as we're more interested in how it will be packaged. The important points are:

- We load the starting page then follow links through to other pages and process these recursively to build up the entire ToC

- We only follow links to more specific URLs than the current page (that is, subpaths), so we don't get into infinite loops

- At each level, we load all child pages in parallel and use `Promise.all` to combine the results

We'll also add a simple module to print a ToC to the console, as given in `consolePrinter.js`:

```
'use strict';
const printEntry = function(entry, indent) {
        console.log(`${indent} - ${entry.name} (${entry.url})`);
        entry.children.forEach(childEntry => {
            printEntry(childEntry, indent + '  ');
        })
    }

module.exports = toc => printEntry(toc, '');
```

# Defining an npm package

To define an npm package, we must add a file to act as the entry point to our package. This will just expose the inner modules appropriately, as given in `index.js`:

```
'use strict';
module.exports = require('./autotoc.js');
module.exports.consolePrinter = require('./consolePrinter.js');
```

We also need to add an npm `package.json` file to define our package's metadata. To create this file, you can run `npm init` in the command line and follow the prompts. In our case, the resulting file looks like the following:

```
{
  "name": "autotoc",
  "version": "0.0.1",
  "description": "Automatic table of contents generator for websites",
  "main": "index.js",
  "author": "hgcummings <npmjs@hgc.io> (http://hgc.io/)",
```

```
    "repository": "https://github.com/NodeJsForDevelopers/autotoc",
    "license": "MIT",
    "dependencies": {
      "cheerio": "^0.20.0",
      "denodeify": "^1.2.1",
      "request": "^2.69.0"
    }
}
```

We've used `package.json` files before to specify dependencies for `npm install`. The other fields become much more important when publishing a package to `npm`. Note that we use the `main` property to specify our package's entry point. Actually, `index.js` is the default value, but specifying it explicitly makes this clearer.

# Publishing a package to npm

Once we have defined our package's metadata, publishing it to npm is very straightforward:

- If you do not already have an npm account, create one by running `npm adduser` and specifying a username and password

- Log in using `npm login`

- In the `root` folder of the package, run `npm publish`

That's all we need to do! Our package will now appear in the global npm repository. We can make use of it by (in a new folder) running `npm install autotoc` and writing the following simple demo script as given in `demo.js`:

```
'use strict';
const autotoc = require('autotoc');
autotoc('http://hgc.io')
    .then(autotoc.consolePrinter, err => console.log(err));
```

Running `node demo.js` at the command line produces the following output:

```
NodeJS                                                            —    □    ×
E:\Stuff\projects\nodejs\autotoc>node demo.js
 - Home (http://hgc.io)
   - About (http://hgc.io/about)
   - Speaking (http://hgc.io/speaking)
     - Image credits (http://hgc.io/speaking#credits-ndc2014)
   - Archive (http://hgc.io/archive)
   - Categories (http://hgc.io/categories)
     - .NET (http://hgc.io/categories#.NET-ref)
     - General (http://hgc.io/categories#General-ref)
     - JavaScript (http://hgc.io/categories#JavaScript-ref)
     - Shell (http://hgc.io/categories#Shell-ref)
   - Tags (http://hgc.io/tags)
     - agile (http://hgc.io/tags#agile-ref)
     - bash (http://hgc.io/tags#bash-ref)
     - books (http://hgc.io/tags#books-ref)
     - browserify (http://hgc.io/tags#browserify-ref)
     - c# (http://hgc.io/tags#c#-ref)
     - competitions (http://hgc.io/tags#competitions-ref)
     - gamedev (http://hgc.io/tags#gamedev-ref)
     - grunt (http://hgc.io/tags#grunt-ref)
     - heroku (http://hgc.io/tags#heroku-ref)
     - java (http://hgc.io/tags#java-ref)
     - livereload (http://hgc.io/tags#livereload-ref)
     - maven (http://hgc.io/tags#maven-ref)
     - metaprogramming (http://hgc.io/tags#metaprogramming-ref)
```

# Running automated clients on the web

It's fine to run tools like this against your own website. There are many use cases for this kind of technique. For example, a script that spiders through an entire site and checks every page can be a useful integration/smoke test.

Use cases that involve crawling sites that you don't own require more care. Any public-facing site that you could visit in a browser, you could also access with an automated client like this. But issuing a large number of automated requests against the same host is undesirable. It could be considered poor etiquette at best or a **Denial of Service (DoS)** attack at worst.

Clients should set an appropriate `User-Agent` HTTP header. Some servers might reject requests from clients that don't specify a `User-Agent` or don't appear to be a browser. By convention, crawlers should send a `User-Agent` including the word *bot* in the name and ideally a URL to find out more about the bot. The request library makes it easy to specify headers by passing in an options object. For example:

```
let options = {
  url: 'http://hgc.io',
  headers: {
```

```
    'User-Agent': 'Examplebot/1.0 (+http://example.com/why-im-
crawling-your-website)'
  }
};
request(options).then(...);
```

Crawlers should also check for a `robots.txt` file for each website and respect any rules it contains. See `http://www.robotstxt.org/robotstxt.html` for more information.

Finally, legitimate crawlers of third-party websites should also rate-limit their requests to avoid overwhelming the server.

# Releasing a standalone tool to npm

Some of the `npm` packages we've used so far in this book have been command-line tools rather than libraries, for example Gulp. Creating a command-line tool package is very straightforward. First, we need to define the script that we want people to be able to invoke from the command line, as given in `cli.js`:

```
#!/usr/bin/env node
'use strict';
const autotoc = require('./autotoc.js');
const consolePrinter = require('./consolePrinter.js');
autotoc(process.argv[2])
    .then(consolePrinter, err => console.log(err));
```

This looks much like our demo script from before, with a couple of differences:

- The line at the beginning of the script (called a **shebang line**, starting with `#!`) indicates to the OS that this script should be executed using Node.js
- The URL to crawl is taken from a command-line argument

Now we just need to specify this script in our `package.json`:

```
{
  "name": "autotoc",
  "version": "0.1.1",
  "description": "Automatic table of contents generator for websites",
  "main": "index.js",
  "bin": {
    "autotoc": "./cli.js"
  },
  "author": "hgcummings <npmjs@hgc.io> (http://hgc.io/)",
  "repository": "https://github.com/NodeJsForDevelopers/autotoc",
  "license": "MIT",
```

```
    "dependencies": {
      "cheerio": "^0.20.0",
      "denodeify": "^1.2.1",
      "request": "^2.69.0"
    }
  }
```

To publish our updated package, we first need to update our version number. You can update this in the package directly or use the npm version command, for example

```
> npm version minor
```

This automatically updates the version number to the next major/minor/patch version (as specified) and makes a new git commit with this change.

Since we are already logged into npm, we can now publish the new version of our package by running npm publish again.

We can now make use of our CLI tool as follows (in a new command prompt window):

```
> npm install -g autotoc
> autotoc http://hgc.io
```

# Using Node.js modules in the browser

At the beginning of this chapter, we discussed creating universal modules that can run under Node.js or in the browser. There is another way that we can allow our code to run in both environments.

Browserify (http://browserify.org/) allows you to make use of Node.js modules in the browser. It bundles up your code together with its dependencies. It also provides browser-compatible shims to emulate Node.js built-in modules.

You can install Browserify via npm:

```
> npm install -g browserify
```

Browserify is typically used to package applications. For example, if we wanted to package our demo usage of autotoc from the previous section, we could run:

```
> browserify demo.js -o bundle.js
```

Browserify will create a single JavaScript file containing the code from demo.js, along with its dependencies and transitive dependencies. If we include this in an HTML page, we can now see it working in the browser console:

You can also use Browserify to generate browser-compatible files for individual modules, following the Universal Module Definition pattern discussed earlier in this chapter. For example, to create a UMD version of our `autotoc.js` module from the previous section, we could run:

```
> browserify autotoc.js -s autotoc -o browser/scripts/autotoc.js
```

We could now make use of this via RequireJS. Let's create a simple application that uses autotoc together with jQuery to generate an HTML ToC. First we'll need an HTML file to contain our application and include RequireJS, as given in `browser/index.html`:

```
<!DOCTYPE html>
<head>
    <script data-main="scripts/main"
src="https://cdnjs.cloudflare.com/ajax/libs/require.js/2.1.22/require.
min.js"></script>
</head>
<body>
</body>
```

Now we can implement our application itself, as given in `browser/scripts/main.js`:

```
requirejs.config({
  paths: {
    jquery: 'https://cdnjs.cloudflare.com/ajax/libs/jquery/2.2.1/
jquery.min'
  }
});
require(['autotoc', 'jquery'], function(autotoc, $) {
  'use strict';
  autotoc('http://hgc.io').then(toc => {
    let printEntry = function(entry, parent) {
      let list = $(document.createElement('ul'));
      list.append(
        `<li><a href="${entry.url}">${entry.name}</a></li>`);
      entry.children.forEach(childEntry => {
        printEntry(childEntry, list);
      })
      parent.append(list);
    }

    printEntry(toc, $('body'));
  }, err => console.log(err));
});
```

This results in the following output:

# Controlling Browserify's output

Note that, by default, Browserify generates a bundle of your code and all of its dependencies. Including transitive dependencies, this can result in a very large file. The autotoc module is only 42 lines long, but the generated bundle is over 80,000 lines! Our application above includes both jQuery (via RequireJS) and a version of Cheerio (via Browserify). This is particularly wasteful, since much of Cheerio is a re-implementation of jQuery.

You can instruct Browserify to exclude specific modules and to exclude all external modules. This is particularly useful for third-party modules that follow the UMD pattern. These do not need to be *browserified* and can be excluded from the generated bundle. You can then load them separately in the browser, via an additional script tag or using RequireJS.

For more information on Browserify's usage options, see the official documentation at `https://github.com/substack/node-browserify#usage`.

Browserify provides a lot of flexibility for bundling modules in different ways. It is particularly useful when working on a single codebase with both server-side and client-side functionality. It allows you to write all of your code using Node.js-style modules and to easily share modules between the server and the client.

# Summary

In this chapter, we have written a multi-environment module following the universal module definition pattern, created an npm package for a library and a command-line tool, and packaged Node.js code for the browser using Browserify.

This demonstrates the flexibility of Node.js and the range of use cases for JavaScript and npm beyond just server-side code. In the final chapter, we'll look at the broader context around Node.js. We'll see some of the newer languages and upcoming language features for the platform and how Node.js interacts with other platforms like .NET.

# 14
# Node.js and Beyond

So far, this book has shown you how to work with JavaScript and Node.js in a variety of use cases. In this chapter, we'll look at how the JavaScript ecosystem is continuing to evolve. We'll also see how the .NET and JavaScript ecosystems influence each other and how to integrate them within a single project.

While the chapters so far have aimed to start you on your path into Node.js and JavaScript, this chapter aims to map out the remaining territory. Each of the preceding chapters has provided in-depth step-by-step coverage of a single topic. This chapter will cover a much broader range of topics, with links to resources for further reading.

In this chapter, we will:

- Understand how Node.js and JavaScript are continuing to evolve
- Introduce some of the new and upcoming JavaScript language features
- Look at some alternative programming languages for Node.js and the web
- Consider principles from Node.js that can apply to .NET programming
- See how to integrate Node.js with .NET

## Understanding Node.js versioning

As mentioned in *Chapter 1*, *Why Node.js?*, the release of Node.js v4 in 2015 shows the platform coming to maturity. If you've used Node.js before the end of 2015, you would have seen version numbers such as v0.8.0 or v0.12.0. So why the leap to v4.0.0?

# A brief history of Node.js

Node.js is an open-source project with a corporate sponsor, Joyent. This means that a single company has a lot of influence over the direction of Node.js, but anyone can create their own fork of the source code. This is exactly what happened at the end of 2014. A group of major contributors to Node.js split the project to create a new fork, named **io.js**. A few key properties of io.js were:

- A more open governance model
- A more regular release cycle, keeping more up-to-date with the underlying V8 engine, to take advantage of performance improvements and newer JavaScript language features
- A move to semantic versioning (see `http://semver.org/`), resulting in major version numbers increasing more quickly

Over the course of 2015, the Node.js project reshaped itself to take on the above properties and align with io.js. In September 2015, the release of Node.js v4 brought the two projects back together under a new governance model. Node.js v4 supersedes (and merges) both Node.js v0.12 and io.js v3.3. You can read more about the new governance model at `https://nodejs.org/en/about/governance/`.

# Introducing the Node.js LTS schedule

The timetable for Node.js releases now follows a regular schedule. A new stable release occurs every 6 months. Each stable branch receives fixes as well as new features that reach maturity. The lifetime of stable releases alternates as follows (as shown in the following chart):

- Odd-numbered branches live for 9 months
- Even-numbered branches enter **long-term support** (**LTS**) after 6 months, receiving bug fixes but no new features
- Long-term support lasts for 30 months, with the final 12 months being maintenance mode (critical bug fixes only)

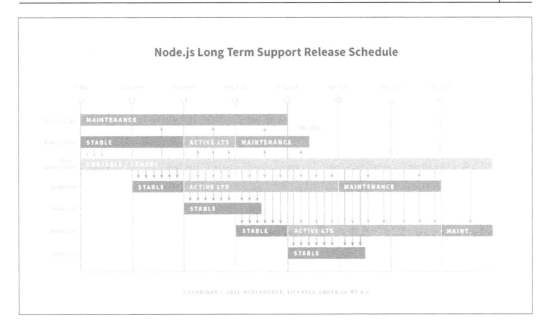

You can find more details of the LTS model at `https://github.com/nodejs/LTS`.

The LTS model allows you to have confidence in Node.js as a platform for your application. The code in this book targets Node.js v6, the current stable release at the time of publication. This version will be in LTS through to April 2019, some three years later.

# Understanding ECMAScript versioning

ECMAScript is the formal standard for the JavaScript language. The first three iterations of the language occurred between 1997 and 1999. A 10-year gap followed before ECMAScript 5 in December 2009. ES5 introduced few new features and focused on cleaning up the language. It introduced strict modes and addressed various inconsistencies, flaws, or gotchas in earlier versions.

2015 saw a major change to the language and to the versioning approach. ECMAScript 2015 (formerly ECMAScript 6) introduced many significant new language features. These include classes, `let`/`const` keywords and block-scoping, arrow functions, and native promises. In the rest of this chapter, we'll look at some of the other significant new features in ES2015.

The name change from ES6 to ES2015 indicates a new yearly versioning model. From 2015 onwards, there will be a new version of the ECMAScript standard every year. Planned features that aren't quite ready for release will wait until the following year. For this reason, ECMAScript 2016 is a small release with only a couple of new features.

Note that ECMAScript is the standard and it takes time for new features to be implemented. Indeed, some ES2015 features are still missing from the JavaScript engines in popular browsers. Note though that the major browser vendors are part of the ECMAScript standards process. So browsers, and Chrome's V8 engine (used by Node.js) in particular, should generally not lag too far behind the latest standard.

# Exploring ECMAScript 2015

We have already used many of the new features of ES2015 throughout this book, such as arrow functions, template strings, and promises. We have also already seen ES2015's syntax for classes in *Chapter 3, A JavaScript Primer*.

ES2015 is a major update to the language, including many new features and syntax improvements. This section will cover some of the other useful improvements that we haven't seen so far in the book. For complete coverage of everything new in ES2015, see the excellent *Exploring ES6*, available at `http://exploringjs.com/es6/`.

# Understanding ES2015 modules

As mentioned in previous chapters, ES2015 introduces a new module specification. Recall from *Chapter 4, Introducing Node.js Modules*, that each module system provides the following:

*   A way of declaring a module with a name and its own scope

*   A way of defining functionality provided by the module

*   A way of importing a module into another script

Modules are scoped to their containing file, as in CommonJS. Modules provide functionality via a new `export` keyword. Prefixing an expression with `export` is equivalent to making it a property of the `module.exports` variable in CommonJS. A special `default export` is equivalent to assigning the value of `module.exports` itself. Modules are imported using an `import` keyword rather than a special `require` function. There is one additional restriction: imports must come at the top of the script, before any conditional blocks or other logic.

These might seem like small syntax changes, but they have an important implication. Because defining and importing modules doesn't involve assignment and method calls, the structure of dependencies between modules is static. This allows the JavaScript engine to optimize loading of modules (particularly important in the browser). It also means that cyclic dependencies between modules can be resolved.

You can find out more about the new ES2015 module syntax at `http://jsmodules.io/`.

# Using syntax improvements from ES2015

In this section we'll look at some of the new syntax features in ES2015 that we haven't used in the book so far. These are all available in the latest JavaScript engines, including Node.js v6.

## The for... of loop

Let's say we have an array defined as follows:

```
let myArray = [1, 2, 3];
```

Let's also say that another library has added a helper function to all arrays. Perhaps something like our `flatMap` function from *Chapter 13, Creating JavaScript Packages*.

```
Array.prototype.flatMap = function(callback) {
    return Array.prototype.concat.apply([], this.map(callback));
};
```

If you wanted to iterate through all the members of an array, you might be tempted to use JavaScript's `for... in` construct as follows:

```
for (let i in myArray) {
    console.log(myArray[i]);
}
```

This doesn't work very well though, as it includes properties on the array's prototype and prints out the `flatMap` function as well as the elements in the array. This is a common problem with `for... in` loops, when used with objects as well as with arrays. The standard way to avoid it is by skipping prototype properties as follows:

```
for (let i in myArray) {
    if (myArray.hasOwnProperty(i)) {
        console.log(myArray[i]);
    }
}
```

This prints out just the elements of the array, as we want. A similar loop could also be used to print the properties of an object, without accidentally attempting to print out functions from the prototype (which may have been added by a third-party library).

Note that `for...` `in` also doesn't technically guarantee the order in which it iterates through the keys of an object. This means it's not really the best thing to use with arrays, where we expect a specific order. That's why the standard way to iterate through arrays is using a plain old `for` loop, as follows:

```
for (let i = 0; i < myArray.length; ++i) {
    console.log(myArray[i]);
}
```

ES2015 addresses these issues with a new `for...` `of` loop, which looks like this:

```
for (let value of myArray) {
    console.log(value);
}
```

The syntax is very similar to `for...` `in` loops. However, you do not need to filter out prototype members as these are excluded. It can be used with any iterable objects (such as arrays) and will follow the natural ordering of the iterable. In short, `for...` `of` loops are like `for...` `in` loops but without any nasty surprises.

## The spread operator and rest parameters

The **spread operator** allows you to treat arrays as if they were a sequence of values. For example, to call a function:

```
let myArray = [1, 2, 3];
let myFunc = (foo, bar, baz) => (foo + bar) * baz;
console.log(myFunc(...values)); // Prints 9
```

You can also use the spread operator within array literals, for example:

```
let subClauses = ['2a', '2b', '2c'];
let clauses = ['1', '2', ...subClauses, '3'];
    // Equivalent to ['1', '2', '2a', '2b', '2c', '3']
```

The **rest parameter** syntax serves the opposite purpose, turning a sequence of values into an array. This is similar to the `params` keyword in C# or `varargs` in Java. For example:

```
function foldLeft(combine, initial, ...values) {
    let result = initial;
    for (let value of values) {
        result = combine(result, value);
```

```
    }
    return result;
}
console.log(foldLeft((x, y) => x+y, 0, 1, 2, 3, 4)); // Prints 10
```

# Destructuring assignment

**Destructuring** allows you to use structuring syntax to assign multiple variables together. For example, you can assign variables using the array literal syntax to destructure arrays:

```
let foo, bar;
[foo, bar] = [1, 2]; // Equivalent to foo = 1, bar = 2
```

You can also combine destructuring with the spread operator:

```
[foo, bar, ...rest] = [1, 2, 3, 4, 5];
    // Equivalent to foo = 1, bar = 2, rest = [3, 4, 5]
```

Finally, you can use destructuring with the object literal syntax:

```
{ foo, bar } = { foo: 1, bar: 2 }; // Equivalent to foo=1, bar=2
```

Destructuring is particularly useful for dealing with complex return values. Imagine if any of the expressions on the right-hand side of the equals sign in the above examples were actually function calls.

Destructuring is also useful for performing multiple assignments in a single statement. For example:

```
[foo, bar] = [bar, foo]; // Swap foo and bar in place
[previous, current] = [current, previous + current];
    // Calculation step for a Fibonacci sequence
```

# Introducing generators

ES2016 introduces **generator functions** and the `yield` keyword. You may already be familiar with the `yield` keyword in C#. Methods that return `IEnumerable`/`IEnumerator` can include the `yield` keyword to return one element at a time, suspending execution of the method until the next value is requested. You can do the same with generator functions in JavaScript. The following example is a JavaScript implementation of one of the examples from the MSDN documentation of C#'s `yield`. It prints the first eight powers of 2 (note the asterisk after the function keyword, which denotes this as a generator function):

```
'use strict';
function* powers(number, exponent) {
```

```
        let result = 1;
        for (let i = 0; i < exponent; ++i) {
            result = result * number;
            yield result;
        }
    }
    for (let i of powers(2, 8)) {
        console.log(i);
    }
```

Note that `for... of` loops work with generators. The above loop is equivalent to the following code:

```
let generator = powers(2, 8);
let current = generator.next();
while (!current.done) {
    console.log(current.value);
    current = generator.next();
}
```

You can see that generators are very similar to the `IEnumerator` interface in C#. Note that they are slightly more powerful than this though. We can also pass a value *into* a generator's `next` method to allow it to be used when execution continues in the generator function. The following dummy example illustrates this:

```
'use strict';
function* generator() {
    let received = yield 1;
    console.log(received);
    return 3;
}
let instance = generator();
let first = instance.next();
console.log(first);
let last = instance.next(2);
console.log(last);
```

Running the previous example produces the following output:

```
> { value: 1, done: false }
> 2
> { value: 3, done: true }
```

This two-way communication makes generators much more than just `IEnumerator` for JavaScript. They are a powerful control flow mechanism, especially when combined with promises. See `https://www.promisejs.org/generators/` for a derivation of C#-like `async`/`await` functionality using generators and promises (with `yield` taking the place of C#'s `await` keyword). It's also worth noting that `async` functions are planned for a future version of ECMAScript (probably ES2017) and will work in a similar way. In the meantime, you can achieve a similar programming model using the `Promise.coroutine` method provided by the bluebird library, which is based on generators. See `http://bluebirdjs.com/docs/api/promise.coroutine.html` for details.

# Introducing ECMAScript 2016

As mentioned earlier in this chapter, ECMAScript 2016 is a small release with only a couple of new features. These are an `includes` method for arrays and the exponentation operator `**`.

You can write `myArray.includes(value)` instead of `myArray.indexOf(value)` `!== -1`. Note that these expressions are not quite equivalent. You can use `includes` to check for the value `NaN` within an array, which you can't do with `indexOf`.

The exponential operator allows you to rewrite `Math.pow(coefficient, exponent)` as `coefficient ** exponent`.

You can also combine it with an assignment, as in `myVariable **= 2`.

# Going beyond JavaScript

If you want to target browsers or Node.js, JavaScript is the only language natively supported by these environments. This is different to VM-based environments like the .NET runtime and the JVM, which support multiple languages.

The .NET runtime supports C#, F#, VB.NET, and others. The JVM supports Java, Scala, Clojure, and others. These languages work by compiling down to an assembly language for the environment's VM. This is the Common Intermediate Language in .NET or Java bytecode in the case of the JVM.

There is a reason why programmers don't all write CIL or Java bytecode though. These are low-level machine languages and much less human-friendly than C#, Java, and so on. In general, higher-level languages can support better productivity, as well as safety (for example, through type systems and memory management).

There is also a reason why .NET programmers don't always use C# and JVM programmers don't always use Java. A range of languages can serve different use cases better. It can also just be a matter of personal taste for the semantics of a particular language.

JavaScript has been called the *Assembly Language for the Web* (`http://www.hanselman.com/blog/JavaScriptIsAssemblyLanguageForTheWeb SematicMarkupIsDeadCleanVsMachinecodedHTML.aspx`). While JavaScript is not a low-level or machine language, it is a common language for its platform. Like CIL and Java bytecode, it can serve as a compile target for other languages. And, like .NET and the JVM, there is an appetite amongst developers for a variety of languages on the same platform.

# Exploring compile-to-JavaScript languages

There are several languages that support web and Node.js development by compiling down to JavaScript. We'll look at a few of the more prominent of these languages in this section.

## TypeScript

The TypeScript language is developed and supported by Microsoft. Its key aim is to include features that aid large-scale application development. TypeScript can be compiled down to ES2016, ES5, or even ES3. So it works in any modern JavaScript environment.

TypeScript is based closely on the JavaScript syntax. It is a superset of JavaScript, so you can write ordinary JavaScript and gradually use TypeScript features more as you learn it. TypeScript also tries to match the syntax of upcoming JavaScript features where possible. This allows developers to start using new JavaScript features earlier.

The most important TypeScript features aid large-scale application development. TypeScript has had classes and modules for some time, to help with structuring code. As the name suggests, TypeScript also adds type annotations and type inference. It also adds new ways of defining and specifying types, including enums, generic types, and interfaces. This makes for a safer language as the compiler can catch more errors. It also lets IDEs offer features like code completion (namely, Intellisense) and better source code navigation.

Finally, TypeScript makes it possible to specify type definitions for libraries written in plain JavaScript. Type definitions for many third-party libraries can be found at `https://github.com/DefinitelyTyped/DefinitelyTyped`. These provide type checking and code completion when working with library code too.

Here's an example of our `flatMap` function from the previous chapter written with type annotations:

```
function flatMap<T, R>(
    source:T[],
    callback:(T)=>R[]): R[] {
    return Array.prototype.concat.apply([],
        source.map(callback));
}
let result = flatMap([1, 2, 3], (i:number) => [i, i + 0.5]);
console.log(result); // Prints [1, 1.5, 2, 2.5, 3, 3.5]
```

The syntax for generics may be familiar from C#. Type annotations follow the expression or parameter, separated by a colon. We could specify the generic type when we call the function too, but in this case it can be inferred. Note that our method has two generic types, as our callback could map to an array of a different element type. The TypeScript compiler will infer the type of `result` as `number[]`. Note that this inference actually takes a few steps:

- We specify that the `callback` parameter i has a type `number`
- Therefore, the expressions i and i + 0.5 also both have a type `number`
- Therefore, the result type of our `callback` is `number[]`
- Therefore, the argument for the type parameter R must be `number`

If we did not specify the type of i, then the compiler would only infer the type of `result` as `any[]`, that is an array, but of an unspecified element type.

You can learn more about TypeScript at `http://www.typescriptlang.org/`.

 If you're more familiar with Java than .NET, and especially if you're familiar with the Eclipse IDE in particular, you may also be interested in N4JS (`http://numberfour.github.io/n4js/`). This language has similar goals to TypeScript, but is inspired by Java and has an IDE based on Eclipse.

# CoffeeScript

CoffeeScript was one of the earliest successful compile-to-JavaScript languages. CoffeeScript streamlines the syntax of JavaScript and adds features for writing more terse and expressive code.

CoffeeScript is a good example of when taste might influence language choice. Developers may find CoffeeScript more readable and/or easier to write. Ruby or Python programmers may be particularly comfortable with CoffeeScript. They'll find its syntax and many of its language features familiar.

Many features from CoffeeScript have subsequently appeared in ES2015, for example arrow functions, destructuring, and the splat/spread operator. Unlike TypeScript, CoffeeScript does not attempt to match the syntax of JavaScript, neither for current nor upcoming features. It does however offer seamless interoperability with JavaScript code.

Comprehensions are one of CoffeeScript's most expressive features and do not appear in ES2015. You may be familiar with comprehensions from Python. They are also a little like LINQ in C#, in that they allow you to express operations on lists without using loops. The following example prints the squares of even numbers, first in JavaScript and then as a one-liner in CoffeeScript. As `squares.js`:

```
var i, n;
for (n = i = 1; i <= 10; n = ++i) {
    if (n % 2 === 0) {
        console.log(n * n);
    }
}
```

As `squares.coffee`:

```
console.log n*n for n in [1..10] when n%2 is 0
```

# And beyond...

TypeScript and CoffeeScript are specifically designed to target JavaScript. There are many other projects in existence that allow more general languages to compile JavaScript. Note that not all such projects are mature or well-maintained. Languages whose own project team supports and maintains compilation to JavaScript tend to be a safer choice. Both Dart (`https://www.dartlang.org/`) and Clojure (`http://clojure.org/`) provide first-class support for compiling to JavaScript.

# Introducing a true assembly language for the web

As discussed above, while JavaScript can be a common compile target for the web and Node.js, it is not a true assembly language. It is a high-level human-readable language, rather than an optimized machine language. There are projects to introduce just such a language into the web environment though. This means defining an assembly language implemented by all browsers, including Chrome's V8 engine and therefore Node.js.

## Understanding asm.js

The first attempt at such a language is asm.js (`http://asmjs.org/`), developed by Mozilla. This is a strict subset of JavaScript, which means it can run on any browser. But browsers that support asm.js can precompile it and heavily optimize its execution. Demanding applications such as 3D games can be recompiled to target asm.js and run seamlessly in-browser. The first environment with full support for asm.js is Mozilla's own Firefox browser. It will also be supported in Microsoft's new Edge browser. The V8 engine used by Chrome (and Node.js) does not yet pre-compile asm.js, but V8 does make some optimizations to allow asm.js to run much faster than if interpreted as plain JavaScript.

## Understanding WebAssembly

WebAssembly (`https://webassembly.github.io/`) is a new standard for a true assembly language for the web. Unlike asm.js it is not a subset of JavaScript and won't run in today's browsers. It defines a new assembly language more like CIL or Java bytecode. It is developed by the W3C standards body, with input from the major browser vendors. There are early implementations of WebAssembly in preview releases of Mozilla Firefox, Google Chrome, and Microsoft Edge.

As an application developer, you do not need to be able to write WebAssembly any more than you need to write CIL or Java bytecode. These are all low-level languages to act as compilation targets. In future, WebAssembly may replace JavaScript as the common compile target for the web (and Node.js). Other languages, including JavaScript itself, may all compile to WebAssembly.

This would mean that JavaScript would no longer be the only native language for the web and Node.js. But JavaScript will almost certainly remain the default development language for these environments, just as C# and Java are for their respective environments. Knowledge of the execution model of Node.js will still be relevant in any language and JavaScript will still be the most natural fit for this execution model. Knowledge of JavaScript will also be important for working with the many well-established libraries based on it.

There would be other benefits to JavaScript from WebAssembly. Interoperation between JavaScript and other languages will become easier. There will be more options for implementing performance-critical code. New versions of JavaScript will be able to roll out more quickly (as a single JavaScript to WebAssembly compiler can target all browser engines).

# JavaScript and ASP.NET

On the server side, we don't need to wait for WebAssembly to mature in order to work with Node.js and .NET together. There is already some convergence between programming on these two platforms and support for interoperability between them.

# Exploring .NET Core

The next version of NET, called .NET Core, makes some major changes to the platform. Some of these changes might seem familiar if you've spent some time working with Node.js. This is not just a coincidence. Microsoft are incorporating good ideas that have worked in Node.js and elsewhere into their ecosystem.

## Defining project structure in .NET Core

.NET Core separates the programming platform from the IDE. Microsoft still recommends using Visual Studio, but have made it much easier to use other editors. For example, the OmniSharp project (`http://www.omnisharp.net/`) supports development in other editors, providing features such as Intellisense outside of Visual Studio.

One aspect of this change is simplifying the use of `.csproj` files. In previous versions of .NET, these large XML files were the canonical description of each C# project. They included important things like compilation options, target platforms, build steps, and dependencies. They were mainly generated by Visual Studio, difficult to edit by hand, and often particularly awkward to merge in source control. To satisfy Visual Studio, they also needed to list every single source file in the project.

Many of these drawbacks are addressed in .NET Core. New tools make it much easier to edit `.csproj` files from the command line. A project's sources are just the files under its parent folder (not listed in `.csproj` or any other metadata file). Dependencies are declared separately in a more lightweight JSON-based file.

Many of these improvements are inspired by programming platforms like Node.js. In fact, early release candidates for .NET Core removed the need for `.csproj` files entirely and introduced `project.json` files (just like in Node.js) for defining projects. Although .NET Core ultimately uses `.csproj` files (for continued compatibility with MSBuild), it aims to keep those aspects of more lightweight approaches that are most important to developers.

## Managing dependencies in .NET Core

The NuGet package manager has been part of the .NET ecosystem for several years. NuGet becomes even more important in .NET Core. The framework and runtime themselves are distributed as NuGet packages. Dependencies are specified as NuGet package names (and versions) rather than DLL paths. NuGet packages can also be a useful unit of deployment for your own projects.

Just like with Node.js, you can checkout the source code of one of your dependencies to a local folder and reference it there. This allows you to tinker with open source libraries and debug them as part of your program.

## Building web applications in ASP.NET Core

ASP.NET Core consolidates ASP.NET MVC and WebAPI into a single framework. It also brings OWIN to the fore as the standard abstraction for implementing web applications.

OWIN simply defines a standard for passing request and response objects between a host and an application. Although OWIN has been around for a while and has its own history, this is a similar abstraction to the `http.createServer` method in Node.js. You can read more about OWIN at `https://docs.asp.net/en/latest/fundamentals/owin.html`.

Related to this, ASP.NET also uses middleware as the standard building block for web applications. Again, although middleware in .NET has its own history, the abstraction is very similar to middleware in Express. Applications set up a pipeline of middleware, with each having access to the request, response, and the next handler in the chain. Built-in middleware is available for cross-cutting concerns such as authentication, sessions, and routing. You can read more about middleware at `https://docs.asp.net/en/latest/fundamentals/middleware.html`

# Integration with JavaScript

Visual Studio has provided good support for client-side JavaScript development for several years. Microsoft have improved and updated this in the latest versions of ASP.NET and Visual Studio: for example, by including better integration with task runners such as Gulp and Grunt. You can read more about client-side JavaScript support at `https://docs.asp.net/en/latest/client-side/index.html`.

## Server-side JavaScript integration with .NET

The Edge.js project (`https://github.com/tjanczuk/edge`) allows Node.js and .NET to run within the same process. It also defines a very simple way for marshalling method calls between the two. This is much faster than marshalling calls out-of-process (for example, via an HTTP call to a process on the local machine).

Edge.js allows you to take the best of .NET and Node.js. Perhaps you want to use Node.js to put a web interface on top of your existing .NET business logic. Or perhaps you're using Node.js for rapid development of most of your application, but have a particularly CPU-intensive operation that would be easier to optimize in .NET.

Making calls from Node.js to .NET (or vice versa) is very simple. For example, if we have the following .NET class:

```
using System;
using System.Threading.Tasks;
namespace DeepThought
{
  public class UltimateQuestion
  {
    public Task<Object> GetAnswer(object input) {
      var result = new
      {
        description =
          "Answer to The Ultimate Question of " + input,
        value = 42
      };
      return Task.FromResult<object>(result);
    }
  }
}
```

We can use it from JavaScript as follows (after running `npm install edge`):

```
'use strict';
const edge = require('edge');
let getAnswer = edge.func({
    assemblyFile: 'bin\\Debug\\DeepThought.dll',
    typeName: 'DeepThought.UltimateQuestion',
    methodName: 'GetAnswer'
});
getAnswer('Life, the Universe, and Everything', (error, result) =>
{
    console.log(result);
});
```

Compiling our C# code and running our JavaScript file results in the following output:

```
> node index.js
> { description: 'Answer to The Ultimate Question of Life, the Universe,
and Everything', value: 42 }
```

You can find a good introduction to Edge.js at `http://www.hanselman.com/blog/ItsJustASoftwareIssueEdgejsBringsNodeAndNETTogetherOnThreePlatforms.aspx`.

Finally, recall that the OWIN standard and ASP.NET middleware are quite similar to the corresponding concepts in JavaScript. Edge.js makes it easy to include a .NET OWIN application as middleware in a Node.js Express application. See the `connect-owin` project at `https://github.com/bbaia/connect-owin` for details.

# Summary

In this chapter, we have seen how Node.js and JavaScript's new release cycles bring stability to the platform. We have introduced some of the new and upcoming features of JavaScript. We have explored current and future alternative languages for the JavaScript environment. We have seen some of the commonalities between .NET and Node.js and how to use these technologies together.

I hope this book has allowed you to get up-and-running with Node.js and given you an appetite to learn more. The resources in this chapter will help you take the next step on your journey with JavaScript and Node.js.

# Index

## Symbol

**.NET Core**
  about  216
  dependencies, managing  217
  project structure, defining  216
  web applications, building  217

## A

**adapter pattern  139**
**afterEach hook  61**
**aggregation pipeline  114**
**Ajax**
  used, for communication  44-47
**alternative session stores**
  using  170
**AMD modules**
  using, with RequireJS  190, 191
**app.js file  13**
**application**
  deploying, with Heroku  159, 160
  executing, locally with Heroku  158, 159
**application framework**
  Express, using  11, 12
  using  10, 11
**array literal notation  24**
**asm.js file**
  about  215
  URL  215
**ASP.NET**
  .NET Core  216
  and JavaScript  216
  integration, with JavaScript  218
  server-side JavaScript integration  218, 219
**assembly language**
  about  215

asm.js  215
  WebAssembly  215
**assertions**
  writing, with Chai  61-63
**asynchronous code**
  callback pattern, using  92
  operations, parallelizing with
      promises  105, 106
  promise-based asynchronous code,
      implementing  101, 102
  writing, promises used  99-101
**asynchronous interfaces**
  consuming  95-98
**Asynchronous Module Definition
      (AMD)  188**
**asynchronous programming**
  about  3
  patterns, combining  106, 107
**asynchronous tests**
  writing, in Mocha  69

## B

**BDD-style tests**
  state, resetting  60, 61
  writing, with Mocha  57-59
**beforeEach hook  61**
**behavior-driven development
      (BDD) style  57**
**binary JSON (BSON)  110**
**browser**
  Node.js modules, using  198-200
**Browserify**
  output, controlling  201
  URL  198, 201
**build process**
  automating, with Gulp  80

tests, executing with Gulp 80, 81

www.ingramcontent.com/pod-product-compliance
Lightning Source LLC
Chambersburg PA
CBHW060542060326
40690CB00017B/3581